William C. Bradstreet

William C. Bradstreet

SCENERY

◀ Sketch for the Monastery Setting, in Cushing's "The Devil in the
◀ Cheese," Stanford University. Designed by Harold Helvenston

SCENERY

A manual
of scene
design

By HAROLD HELVENSTON

Director of Dramatics
Stanford University

1931
Stanford University Press
Stanford University, California
London: Humphrey Milford
Oxford University Press

STANFORD UNIVERSITY PRESS
STANFORD UNIVERSITY, CALIFORNIA

LONDON: HUMPHREY MILFORD
OXFORD UNIVERSITY PRESS

THE BAKER & TAYLOR COMPANY
55 FIFTH AVENUE, NEW YORK

MARTINUS NIJHOFF
9 LANGE VOORHOUT, THE HAGUE

THE MARUZEN COMPANY
TOKYO, OSAKA, KYOTO, SENDAI

COPYRIGHT 1931 BY THE BOARD OF TRUSTEES
OF THE LELAND STANFORD JUNIOR UNIVERSITY

PRINTED AND BOUND IN THE UNITED STATES
OF AMERICA BY STANFORD UNIVERSITY PRESS

To George Pierce Baker

FOREWORD

THERE are two occasions when I regret the hundreds of thousands of words I have written on the new stagecraft in the past twenty years. One of these is when I see a Broadway production in which a brilliant, imaginative, but selfish and undisciplined scene designer has been allowed to run away with a play and ruin it through some original, wrong-headed, and thoroughly inappropriate treatment. The other occasion is when I see a little-theatre production in which the scenery is workmanlike or even brilliant and the acting abominable.

In the first case I am righteously outraged at a scenic crime. In the second the chances are that I myself am committing the crime: I am laying upon a sound workman in scenery some of the blame for a bad performance by directors and actors. Of course it may be that in certain cases the actors are neglected to make a scenic holiday, but the chances are that the acting talent is inherently hopeless and that I ought to be glad to have my attention diverted by the silent art of color and light. At any rate we can't stop good scene design among the amateurs. It is the one thing at which the little theatre can always excel, because it is at bottom a one-man product. One actor can't make a good cast, but one artist, one architect, or one interior decorator can always make a good setting. If he studies—

And here is something for him to study. The contribution of Harold Helvenston—and I think a foreword may point the values of a book without stepping over into criticism—is that here at last we have a first-rate designer writing a practical manual. Therefore it is a nice combination of theory and practice. Not too much of high-flown generalities; not too much of technical details. It rides no hobbies and points no exclusive patent way to aesthetic salvation. It is open-minded toward both realism and expressionism. It leaves to experience and the teacher-specialist numerous technical matters, such as the method of enlarging sketch-designs to backdrop proportions, the construction of flats, the varieties of spotlights and projection machines.

The reader may be trusted to discover the practical virtues of this book; and they range from the salutary ignoring of "drape productions" to a careful reiteration that the designer paints his scenery twice, once with pigment and once with light, before it approximates the colors of his original sketch.

As a theatre man who lives and works in a part of the United States where most of the seats of higher education are a bit backward in the teaching of the arts of the theatre, I want to close by stressing the significance of this book in relation to university instruction. It is printed and published by a university. It is written by a teacher in a university, who is at the same time a designer taught by a university. It is illustrated by the work of teachers and students. Because or in spite of this—let your prejudice decide, as it always does—this manual seems all in a key of practicality and safe accomplishment. Anyone who reads it may go farther. No one who follows it can arrive at less than a just expression of his talents.

KENNETH MACGOWAN

PREFACE

This book does not presume to offer aid to the professional. It is designed for the amateur interested in the problems and technique of scene design, more particularly for use in little theatres, high schools, universities, and dramatic clubs where the efforts of the designer are usually governed by a definite and limited budget and where the general tendency is to use stock settings, makeshift scenery, or "just a few drapes," instead of a suitable and well-designed stage setting for each individual play. In a nutshell, the purpose of the book is to offer a process for the development of stage settings suitable to the play and in keeping with the production, with an eye toward good taste and strict economy.

I am deeply indebted to Donald Mitchell Oenslager, Stanley McCandless, and Philip Barber, of the Yale University Department of the Drama for their expert instruction and for their exacting demands, which taught me to be careful, and for the inspiration gained while a student in their classes. I am particularly grateful to Professor Lee Emerson Bassett and Mr. Gordon Davis for their encouragement and invaluable suggestions; to Mr. Charles G. Norris for his unfailing interest in the book; to Dr. Margery Bailey, Mr. Barrett H. Clark, Mr. Robert Cathcart, and Mr. John McClelland for their work and assistance in reading the manuscript; to Edwin H. Smith for financial data; to Miss Alma Steininger, Mr. Frederick Stover, Mr. Frank Poole Bevan, Mr. Arthur Hurt, Mr. William Kline, and others, whose sketches appear within the book; and last, but not least, to the staff of Stanford University Press, whose enthusiasm and care are evidenced in the making of the book.

To assume that the book is all-inclusive or altogether complete would be to put it in a false light. Neither is it to be regarded as an infallible collection of the "only methods" of doing things scenically—it is simply a method for the evolution of the stage setting through its many phases, written from the point of view of a plan that has worked.

HAROLD HELVENSTON

PALO ALTO, CALIFORNIA
March 18, 1931

CONTENTS

	PAGE
Foreword by Kenneth Macgowan	ix
List of Illustrations	xv
Scenery and the Designer	3
A Process for Scene Design	11
A Process for Scene Design—Working Drawings	17
A Process for Scene Design—The Scene Model	32
Light in the Scene	38
Scene Painting	51
The Exterior Scene—The Natural Exterior	61
The Exterior Scene—The Architectural Exterior	68
Economy in Cost of Construction and Materials	72
The Strange Case of Scenery	79
The Scene Webster	83
Index	91

ILLUSTRATIONS

	PAGE
Sketch for the monastery setting in Cushing's "The Devil in the Cheese"	*Frontispiece*
Model of setting for Toller's *Masse Mensch*	4
The same setting with different lighting	4
Setting for Karel Čapek's *The Makropolous Secret*	5
Scene from Bernard Shaw's *Pygmalion*	5
Sketch for Act One of S. Ansky's *The Dybbuk*—a synagogue in Brainitz	6
Sketch for Act Two showing contrast of poverty and riches	6
Sketch for Act Three—a setting for mystic atmosphere	7
Scene from the second act, the design enhancing the mood	7
A setting for a piano duet in a musical revue	12
A setting from J. Wong-Quincey's *Peking Politics*	13
Another setting using the same scenic unit with different lighting	13
Sketch for a scene in Bernard Shaw's *Saint Joan*, using distortion for effect	14
Design for *The Last of the Lowries* by Paul Green	14
Sketch of a unit arrangement for Swinburne's *Chastelard*	15
Sketch for "The Tower" scene, using units with removable panels	16
Floor plan showing arrangement of stage and scenic details	18
Drawing to show application of the theory of sight lines	20
Sectional view of auditorium and stage, showing sight lines from the balcony	20
Drawing of an elevation showing details of a Pullman car setting	21
Drawing of a cross-section of a Pullman car setting; to scale	21
Simplified realistic setting for Ibsen's *Brand*	22
Setting for Stanford University production of *The Makropolous Secret*	24
A scene from *Peking Politics*, showing scale of furniture	25

	PAGE
Stage setting from *Peking Politics*, showing simplicity of design	26
Another setting from *Peking Politics*, of simple design	27
Scene sketch for setting from Stanford University production of Ibsen's *Wild Duck*	30
Photograph of actual setting made from previous sketch	30
Sketches showing the evolution of stage settings	31
Sketch for ship setting in *Tristan and Isolde*	31
Sketch for the Epilogue to Bernard Shaw's *Saint Joan*	33
Photograph of model made from the preceding sketch	33
A cardboard model setting for *The Rendezvous of the Unknown Soldier*	34
The same model setting under a different style of lighting	34
Model for *Hamlet*, showing effect produced by the use of miniature stage lighting equipment	35
Another model for *Hamlet*, using miniature stage lighting equipment	35
Model lighting equipment designed by George Hall	36
Model control board for miniature stage lighting	37
A design for a mystery play, suggesting lighting	38
Biblical scene in a Rembrandt painting style	39
Scene from the San Francisco Temple Players' production of *The Dybbuk* with single light source	40
Setting for Priscilla Flowers' *The White Peacock*	41
Setting from the San Francisco Junior League production of *The Sleeping Beauty*	41
Another setting for the same play, showing transparency	41
Sketch for Act One of *The Flying Dutchman*, using dark background	42

SCENERY—A MANUAL OF DESIGN

	PAGE
Sketch for another scene in the same act, with light projections	42
Scene from *Creation*, a mechanistic ballet, showing use of spotlight	43
An example of overhead lighting in a scene from the Bohemian Club's Christmas Play of 1930	45
A setting from Littleton's *Pueblo* as produced at the Yale University Theatre	46
Another setting from the same play illustrating the use of structural units	46
The graveyard setting for Elmer Rice's *The Adding Machine*, with special proscenium arch	47
Sketch for Clemence Dane's *Granite*, with obvious lighting	47
A scene from *The Singing Minute* by Maude Humphrey, with detail characteristic of realistic type of setting	48
A scene from the Stanford University production of Karel Čapek's *The Makropolous Secret*	50
A sketch for the Stanford University production of Evreinov's *The Chief Thing*, in amusing design	51
Sketch for 1927 Fine Arts Ball at Yale, giving atmosphere of merriment	53
A scene from Priscilla Flowers' *The White Peacock*, using painted scenery on the back of flats	54
Setting for Pirandello's *Right You Are*	56

	PAGE
Setting for a circus operetta, using hinged flats	56
Rococo setting for Sherwood's *The Queen's Husband*, as produced at Stanford University	57
Setting for Michael Rafetto's Christmas Play for the Bohemian Club of San Francisco, with neutral background	58
Sketch showing method of painting architectural detail	59
A scene from Milne's *The Ivory Door*	60
A proposed scene for O'Neill's *The Emperor Jones*	61
A garden setting for Robert Powell's *Brief Candle*	64
Design for the tropical island setting of Cushing's *The Devil in the Cheese*	65
An exterior setting for Talbot Jennings' *No More Frontier*	69
Setting for Grace Dorcas Ruthenberg's *Retreat*, an example of realistic architectural exterior	70
An architectural interior for *Wings over Europe* by Robert Nichols and Maurice Browne	70
Sketch for W. Hasenclever's *Wanted: A Gentleman*, suggesting a park scene	73
Setting for Katherine Clugston's *Finished*	74
Design for a backdrop for jazz music, with abstract treatment	74
Design for a backdrop in a musical revue, using the human face as motif	75

SCENERY

SCENERY AND THE DESIGNER
Scenery in Play Production

SCENERY contributes to dramatic production by creating an atmospheric background for the play and by intensifying the dominant emotional character of the scene. It may be called the advance agent for the play, sent out ahead at the rise of the curtain in order to produce psychological, emotional, and aesthetic effects upon the group mind of the audience.

The form of drama is usually established by the character of the setting when the first curtain goes up. Certain physical lines, the lights, the shadows, and the somber tones of a setting may well convey the tragic quality of a serious play; other lines, lights and shadows, brightness, color, and warmth may easily suggest the airy and lighter mood of comedy; while the physical oddities of still another setting may readily give the atmosphere expected in a mystery play. The setting in this way establishes in the audience's mind the form of the drama and heralds the action that follows.

The stage setting also suggests the style of production. The producer's attitude toward both the play and the audience must be conveyed by setting. Realistic or naturalistic representation prepares the way for a similar treatment of the play and similar direction of the actors. Suggested detail or complete abstraction in a setting might proclaim in advance the expressionistic style of director and artist and a radical departure from the play or the original style of its production. The Hopkins-Jones production of *Macbeth* in America and the Hilar production of *Hamlet* in Germany offer two examples of expressionistic stage presentation. In the first, the designer used stylized shapes and masks representative of the mood and spirit of the tragedy; in the latter, the focality of the actor was gained by the use of simple but effective screens as backgrounds. Another director, by a skeleton arrangement of stairways, ramps, and platforms, seeks to inform his audience at the first that he visualizes the play in a constructivistic manner; the scenes of the play, in various degrees of action, are heightened by the acting structure, which itself becomes the basis of the visual scene and at all times combines with the moving silhouetted forms of the actors to form the spectacle.

As a whole, scenery may be used to augment the ideas of the producer, and thus it becomes an advance agent of his own particular style. This use of scenery has, for the past few years, become generally known to orthodox playgoers.

A degree between the extremes of realism and abstraction may be skilfully used to predict the special qualities of the varied scenes, particularly in plays that present such problems as a state of mind or a personal idea of one of the characters—a very popular form for satiric expression. In Cushing's *The Devil in the Cheese* there is a scene of this kind which is described by the words "In Goldina's head"—meaning in this case the thoughts taking place within the mind of the character. A recent and more notable example of this type of scenery was seen in the New York production of Austin Strong's *A Play without a Name,* in which the workings of the human brain were presented in scenic illusion. Another example is the production of

SCENERY—A MANUAL OF DESIGN

Eugene O'Neill's *The Emperor Jones*. Half-reality and half-fantasy, the setting here is so important that it occupies the position usually held by an actor; the Emperor is the protagonist; the setting, the forest which breaks down his nerve, is the antagonist. In other plays, such as Elmer Rice's *The Adding Machine* and Ferenz Molnár's *Mima*, scenery is called upon to play a very definite part in the

◀ *Model of constructivist setting for*
◀ *Toller's* Masse Mensch. *Designed by*
◀ *David Rossi while a student at Yale.*

unfolding of the main plot and idea. It may be noted that many such plays have been written in the knowledge that the setting can be employed as a definite factor in the production. Such demands on the part of the dramatist also act as an advance tribute to the ability of the modern scientist of stage scenery.

The definite contributions of scenery that go to make the atmospheric background of a play are locale, time, mood, and aesthetic effect.

Locale, as a term, is usually interpreted to mean geographical location; however, in the case of scenery it should be enlarged so as to include the localizing of personages not only in geographical location but also in social position and rank in life. Locale, in the strict sense of place, is gained by the use of typical forms, colors, and characteristics of the place represented; thus elm trees and Colonial façades may suggest New England; palms and grass huts, a cannibal island; classic colonnades, a square in Athens. Historical period is suggested by significant architectural detail, furniture, and costume. For example: musty, heavy draperies characterize the scene as Victorian; rococo paneling or classic cornices do much to suggest two very different and easily recognizable periods in the social life of France; and, in the same way, a modified Gothic architecture may be used to represent Tudor England. Social position of characters may be indicated in a stage setting by the skilful use of significant decorative detail and, to a great extent, by color and light. A dark and dirty inclosure or a hovel suggests poverty and squalor; a brilliantly lighted formal setting creates the illusion of wealth and splendor; fire escapes, clothes lines, and milk bottles may be used to represent the tenement district of New York; et cetera.

As regards time, the stage setting must be arranged to convey ideas of both season of the year and hour of the day. Season is expressed in a number of ways: fall or winter may be suggested indirectly by the effect of hearth-fire or directly by the color and condition of landscape or foliage; thus, orange and yel-

◀ *The same setting with different light-*
◀ *ing. Note the absence of decorative*
◀ *detail, a characteristic feature of this*
◀ *type.*

low leaves suggest autumn, snow or bare trees indicate winter, and flowers and bright greens symbolize spring or summer. Any of these indications will of necessity be strengthened by suggestive seasonal lighting. Time of day is primarily indicated by lighting, but it is the practice of modern designers to increase the effect by painting the setting itself for light and shadow. This is really the intensi-

—4—

SCENERY AND THE DESIGNER

◀ *The setting for the lawyer's office in the Stanford University production of Karel Čapek's* The Makropolous Secret. *In this setting a great deal of the atmosphere was achieved by design alone. Setting by Harold Helvenston.*

fication of a phenomenon that actually exists. Thus, if a single candle is used in the lighting of a setting, it is effective to paint the illuminated portion around the light-source in lighter and brighter values than the rest; the portion of the ceiling around a chandelier may be represented in lighter tone than that part which is out of the direct range of the

◀ *Scene from the first act of Bernard Shaw's* Pygmalion *as produced at Stanford University. Directed by Harold Helvenston. The grouping of the actors forms probably the most important element of design in the setting.*

SCENERY—A MANUAL OF DESIGN

lighting fixture; and, by the same token, shadows may be made much darker than they really are; all for the sake of theatrical emphasis.

The three sketches shown below were designed by the author of this volume for the San Francisco Temple Players' production of S. Ansky's *The Dybbuk*. These designs emphasize the qualities of mood and atmosphere necessary in stage settings.

Mood is one of the most vital contributions to scenery. The stage setting, in its active service to play and audience, supports not only the emotional mood of the play itself but also the emotional feeling of the actors in individual acts and scenes. It is used to

Sketch for Act One, The Dybbuk. *A synagogue in Brainitz—an evening in winter. The effects of poverty and age have been the keynotes of the designer in this setting.*

Sketch for Act Two. A courtyard of Sender's house in Brainitz—an afternoon in summer. In this scene is shown the contrast of poverty and riches: beggars are exercising their traditional privilege of dancing with the bride.

SCENERY AND THE DESIGNER

augment the effectiveness of special bits of acting, thus forming a valuable aid to the director as well as the actor. This use of scenery becomes an important factor in play an ugly object and show it in a manner uglier than it is, just for sheer emphasis. At any rate, each artist of the scene possesses a power to create in his own terms scenery for

◀ *Sketch for Act Three. Rabbi Azrael's house in Miropol—evening. In*
◀ *this setting a mystic atmosphere has been sought. The wonder-Rabbi*
◀ *is shown in the midst of the ceremony for the exorcism of the evil*
◀ *spirit.*

production. The setting, conceived as mood, amounts to the graphic repetition of the emotional factors of the play and in this way can be used to great advantage by the director. Thus the setting itself forms another aid to the audience's understanding of the play.

The aesthetic effect of a setting is more or less the special touch of the artist in the conception of a production and in turn shows his peculiar stylistic traits in the execution of stage scenery. As a factor, it is almost intangible. The work of a certain artist is immediately identified by special qualities found in his sketch or in the finished setting. Individual differences in the use of line, color, mass, and technique determine the artist's place in the scale of the theatre-goer's appreciation of scene design; thus a certain deft simplicity typifies one artist, an almost careless charm in the grouping of objects signifies another, while the use of light alone proclaims the work of another. With light one artist might make an ordinarily ugly object beautiful in an attempt to represent those qualities in ugliness, while another might take

the stage, and it is by such personal qualities that scenic production offers variety.

In the illustration below from the second act of *The Dybbuk,* note the gnarled, ingrown effect of the architecture, carrying out the mood of the drama.

◀ *Scene from the second act of* The
◀ Dybbuk. *An example of the manner in*
◀ *which the mood of the drama may be*
◀ *enhanced by the design of the setting.*

SCENERY—A MANUAL OF DESIGN

Scenery may be called upon to contribute in many ways, depending a great deal upon the play, the director, and the artist, through the determination and the capacity of each to co-ordinate the production. Since the predominance of any of these factors can usually be detected and is disadvantageous in a production, it is usually best to seek a well-balanced representation of every factor of the play, thus emphasizing the one generally most important element—the play itself.

The Art of the Scene Designer

STAGE design, as it is now practiced, is virtually a new member in the sisterhood of the arts. Certainly never before this modern age has it been common for the multifarious duties of stage designing to be assigned to the artistry of a single individual or, indeed, for a man to devote his entire artistic life to decoration for the stage.

Nicholas Roerich, painter and stage artist, said that all art is indivisible, meaning that no matter what form an artist uses or what medium he employs in the execution of an artistic idea, the result is equally an expression of art. Each example of art represents an attempt by an artist to register for others his own original impression upon feeling, seeing, or hearing something that has seemed wonderful to him.

The work of a sculptor is the result of an inspiration expressed in terms of his own particular medium and technique. A dancer, in an effort to interpret an idea through bodily rhythm, becomes a creator. A caricature is an expression of a search for truth exaggerated in terms of the natural dominant elements found in a subject. An artist-photographer, through his own arrangement of objects, produces a print which is in reality a pictorial idealization of a group of common things. Thus, the sculptor's creation, the dance, the caricature, and the photograph all become expressions of art.

In the modern theatre almost every known art is combined to create a dramatic expression. The arts of literature, the spoken voice, and music combine to affect the auditory senses, while the arts of pantomime, the dance, architecture, sculpture, and painting combine in pictorial illusion to please the eye. The excitement of the auditory and optical senses brings about a third sensation, composite in that it is usually mental and physical in one. Through these various media an audience is impressed.

In an artistic stage production the arts of the theatre are combined in their proper degree of importance and are effectively coordinated into a single dramatic expression. Each element is, in its individual perfection, an integer of dramatic importance to a production. However, it is within the province of this discussion to consider only the scene designer, whose efforts are directed toward bringing about emotional reactions through the visual rather than through the auditory channels.

The designer's qualifications

In former periods scene design was the combined work of architects, painters, and technical engineers; in modern times it is carried on by a single individual who is both artist and craftsman.

A scene designer should possess something of what is called the "soul of the artist." He should instinctively think in terms of visual beauty, sweeping line, and arresting color; and he should be able to register these thoughts in his drawings. Besides displaying imagination in his drawings he must possess skill in the execution of the actual stage setting. He should not be content to inflict upon the public something that is "new" unless the object, in its newness, contains beauty.

For instance, a newly written play is to be produced and an artist is brought in to design the scenes. He carefully reads the script in an effort to understand the main values of the play—to capture the underlying idea. He knows that he must create a special background, and so, steeping himself in the mood of the play, he prepares a number of designs from which final selections are made. The drawings are queer things to one who is not familiar with the play—odd compositions in ghastly colors; one of them is nothing more than the representation of light falling upon the bodies of two men; the scene is apparently, say, a dungeon. After reading the play one sees how the artist has been impressed by the dominant mood of the piece and how he has transferred this feeling into his sketches. Every effort has been made to intensify the atmosphere of ghouls, haunted houses, and marshes at night-time. It is a mystery play, and the artist has expressed the mood of the play in terms of line and color and light. In this way a stage design becomes a graphic expression of emotions—an art all of its own.

The problem of the scene designer is unique. The completion of the pictorial design is only the first step in his work. There are still elevations, details, color charts, and light plots to be prepared, and even after this process the more important work still lies ahead of him—that of executing the actual setting to conform to his sketch. The fact that not all designers paint or execute their own settings signifies nothing. Some may do nothing but design the scenes in sketch form and supervise the painting; others carry the process straight through to the finished setting. However, it is expected that each artist shall be able to interpret his designs and visualize his dream picture in actual wood, canvas, and paint. He must understand every detail of the sketch and must have some idea as to how these effects can be obtained in a physical setting. The designer should have a knowledge of architecture, sculpture, and painting, of costuming, stage lighting, makeup, and various other arts and crafts. Demands upon him are varied and at times strange. His artistry depends a great deal upon his ability to select and combine essential details, and upon his ingenuity in the practical combination of the same scenic units for different scenes. He should spend a great deal of his time experimenting with production materials and technical devices. He should have a working knowledge of the entire process of playmaking and dramatic production and should devote part of his time to the reading of plays and the study of the work of other designers.

The scene designer should never be willing to copy anything of anyone else's, for the theatre is founded upon the principles of self-expression. He should always be open-minded and eager to gain the point of view of other artists, trying always first to analyze a problem and to discover the motivation for another artist's solution to it. In the final analysis it is the combination of an artist's knowledge, his personal aesthetic ideas, and the skill exemplified in his work that provides a basis for his worth in the theatre or for an opinion of his individual art; a scene designer should ever strive to render himself a more efficient artist.

The designer's place in the theatre

The scene designer is the particular artist of the theatre engaged to design and manage the artistic and, sometimes, the technical part of a dramatic production. He is part of an organization of other workers like himself and should always attempt to assist in dramatic production rather than to intrude his individual art to the detriment of the play.

The scene designer must first, last, and always assist the play, the author, and the director. He must interpret the play itself and each scene within the play in a manner conducive to the most expressive action of the play and the greatest intensification of its mood. The scene designer must serve the actors, remembering that he is creating the background for their every movement and that it depends upon his artistic skill whether the visual scenes will be amplified or lessened in effectiveness and sincerity. The background must always be in harmony with the actor; it must never overshadow him or clash with the mood of the scene.

The designer must assist the director in providing the physical ways and means for the play's action. After the director has expressed his desires as to entrances, openings, and physical peculiarities of the setting, it is best for him to allow the designer to execute these special details in his own manner; however, if the director is not pleased with the setting, the artist should be willing to make any necessary revisions. At times the artist is called upon partially or wholly to modify his own ideas in favor of those of the director. In such a case it is always best for the artist to use tact and to maintain a spirit of harmony with the director. Influences other than those of art sometimes affect a director's ideas for a production and its scenes. Above all, there should exist between the director and the artist a perfect understanding, especially in the matter of plans and sketches for settings. After the ideas, plans, and details are accepted by the director, the artist is at liberty to express as much of his personal style in the execution of the settings as he can. It is from this part of the work that the scene designer derives his greatest joy.

A PROCESS FOR SCENE DESIGN
Preliminary Considerations

BEFORE successful scenery can be designed, it is necessary that consideration be given to a number of important factors concerning the play and the conditions relative to its production. This process, undergone long before any work is started on production, forms a prelude to the actual work of the designer. A careful study of such elements results in the creation of stage settings which will be in keeping not only with the financial limitations of the producer or the organization but also with the special conditions of the production and the combination of its various elements into an artistic whole. These considerations may vary according to the character of the working organization of which the designer is a member; however, there are several preliminary factors that govern the scenic production of any theatrical presentation.

The play and the author

The consideration of the script is of primary importance. Determine the type of play immediately. Decide whether it is tragedy, comedy, melodrama, farce, or any of the ordinary forms of drama. If it is musical, place it definitely within its special category, as serious or comic opera, musical comedy, revue, or operetta. It might be a pageant or a tableau. Each of these dramatic forms requires a distinct type of scenic production. Study carefully the author's description of the scenes. Try to grasp the main idea of the play; determine its principal values and the emotional character of each scene. Was the play written in a realistic vein, or is it approached from a symbolic angle? Find out the historical position of the play, either the historical period in which the author has placed the action or, if it is an old play, the literary history of the period in which it was written. Is it modeled after the Greek? Is it approximating Shakespeare? Is it Restoration comedy? Does it belong to any great dramatic era, or is it modern?

It is well to delve into the life of the author and determine the basic influences which caused him to write the play. Study carefully his personal ideas and explanations with relation to his own natural background. This policy is extremely wise and is generally enjoyable to the designer.

The director and the style of production

Consideration of the director is essential if the settings are to be co-ordinated with the proposed action and scheme of the play. Such consideration generally insures harmony between the designer and other members of the production crew. Everyone connected with the production should work toward one specific ideal prescribed by the direction.

Consider the purpose of the production—if there is one. Is it an attempt to produce a play in a manner foreign to its usual style, or is it to be done in an orthodox manner? Is it intended as a production of something classic with little regard for the box-office, or as a commercial venture, pure and simple?

Next determine the nature of the traditional production. How was it done the first time? If it is an old play, try to trace its different productions. Then find out the degree to which the director is adhering to or

— 11 —

departing from the original style of production. Ascertain the director's conception of the script and the general stage directions. Try to get his personal idea of the scenes, the characters, and the details of the play. Discover whether he is directing a realistic play in a realistic manner or is introducing burlesque or farce into his direction for the sake of inspiring fresh interest in a former realistic play. Is he exaggerating the improbable situations of melodrama in the movement and direction of his actors, or is he presenting a special theory or idea he cherishes by doing it in a stylized way?

It is generally conceded that it is wrong to direct a play in one style and to mount it in another. A unity of idea must be expressed through every detail of a dramatic presentation. In the modern theatre it generally follows that the director decides the style of production regardless of tradition and it is up to the designer to co-operate in the execution of stage settings which suit the selected style and enhance the original conception of the director. It is a good policy to try to determine the basic ideas of a production at a joint conference with the director and, whenever possible, with the author; the latter, however, is sometimes not advisable. The director may give his general idea of ground plans and acting areas, a synopsis of necessary detail needed for the business of his actors, and an outline of the ideas he is trying to carry through the production. He may discover that he is able to cut certain scenes or to combine and rearrange scenes so as to obtain greater clarity in unfolding the content of a play and in rendering a script practical for modern production; or he may seek to modify the play in any number of ways according to his own ideas of its production. Such ingenious planning of scenes often furnishes creative opportunity to the designer in the planning of scenery and added ease to the technician in the handling of back-stage scenic units. After such details are decided

◀ *A setting for a piano duet number in a musical review. This could be*
◀ *made in the form of a ground row (a two-way screen hinged in the*
◀ *center and held in position by a stage brace) or it could be painted*
◀ *directly on a back drop. Note also the modification of the proscenium*
◀ *arch. Designed by Harold Helvenston.*

A PROCESS FOR SCENE DESIGN

and thoroughly understood, it remains for the designer to refine these preliminary requirements and suggestions and to create out of them an artistic and adequate background for the play.

The method or style of a dramatic production has a very marked effect upon its scenery. For example, *Hamlet* can be mounted by one producer in settings that are definitely localized and even periodized; another director might want to present this play in a stylistic way, the scenes to take the form of

◀ *A setting from* Peking Politics, *by*
◀ *J. Wong-Quincey, produced at Yale*
◀ *University by George Pierce Baker. Set-*
◀ *tings designed by Harold Helvenston.*

anything from nondescript screens to box-like solids—with no attention to locale and period. In such a production, light might be used as a factor to create scenic pattern. A third type of production might be conceived in a modern manner, with settings typical of the twentieth century and its surroundings. A modern study might be substituted for "A Room in a Castle"; a drawing-room might serve as "A Room of State"; an ordinary field might be employed to suggest "A Plain in Denmark." By this method traditional locale is given up in favor of a novel idea about the play or its characters; a modern period is suggested by means of modern detail. Thus the conception of the director influences the designer in his creation of different types of scenery.

A director might have a certain idea about opening a play and, in thinking of scenic possibilities, might decide to dispute the original scene in an attempt to bring about a greater intensification of the scene itself. In this way Douglas Ross, in his production of *Macbeth*, inspired Gordon Craig to design a bridge as the stage setting for the third scene of Act I. This radical scenic departure was made in an effort to "open the play with a bang." This structure was designated by the director as "The Bridge of Destruction." In this case scenic tradition was ignored in order to emphasize a certain value. The basic conception of the scene was governed by an idea of the director and brought to life according to the aesthetic taste of the designer.

Another director conceived the opening witch scene of *Macbeth* as a visual representation of the ugly spirit of the witches. Light was issued through the eyes of three huge masks hung high above the stage, and shone in a concentrated pool upon the actual witches below. In such a manner, in the modern theatre, many odd and interesting scenes are created as the result of the personal conception of the director and the imaginative genius of the scene designer.

The business manager and the show

The business manager of a producing company is responsible for the budget of the show and for the amount of money appropriated for each element of production. It is through

◀ *Another setting from the same play*
◀ *with different lighting. These settings*
◀ *show how the same scenic unit may*
◀ *be reversed to suggest different scenes.*

the business manager that the designer learns the limitations of expense for the scenic investiture of a dramatic production. Such procedure is almost universal, in commercial

SCENERY—A MANUAL OF DESIGN

organizations, in experimental and little theatres, and in university dramatics. In most instances the designer must consider the budget.

One of the essential duties of the designer is to produce the most effective settings for the least amount of money. Economy is universally recognized as a keynote to successful dramatic production, and it often follows

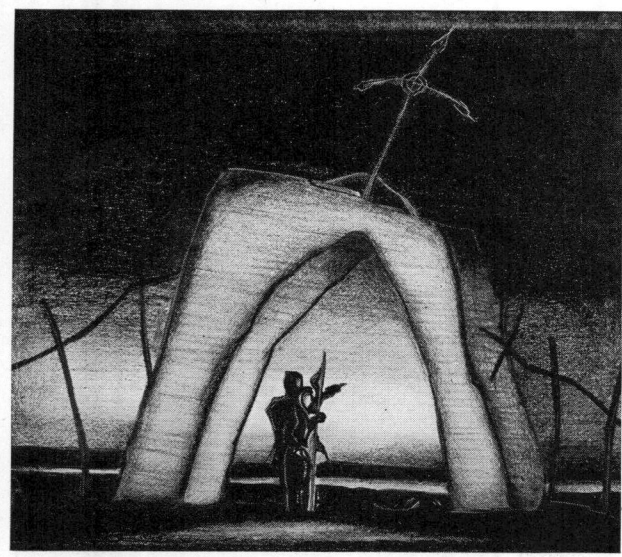

◀ *A sketch for a scene in Bernard*
◀ *Shaw's* Saint Joan, *in which distor-*
◀ *tion is used to gain an impressionistic*
◀ *effect. Designed by Frederick Stover.*

that such necessity upon the part of the scene designer stimulates ingenuity in the discovery and use of appropriate materials for scenic production and also assists the designer in the perfection of his own stylistic technique. The majority of business managers and producers uphold the use of substitutes as one of the primary duties of the designer, and gauge his ability as such in direct proportion to his cleverness in the art of visual deception and his ingenuity in the use of materials.

The type of "draw" or clientèle usually governs the budget and generally determines the degree of elaboration with which a stage setting is executed. If the production is intended for "a class draw" of moneyed patrons artistically inclined, it necessarily follows that the scenery is planned and constructed in a substantial manner, and that the details will be more elaborate and highly finished.

The running period of a show, as antici-pated by the producer and business manager, is an item of direct influence upon the appropriation of money for the scenery of a production. Sometimes the manager foresees the possibilities of taking a show on the road and, in so planning, allows more money for the scenic production. It is obvious that scenery for the road must be stronger in construction and more permanent in its technical arrangement, and thus requires a larger appropriation. Knowledge of such factors is sential to the designer of stage scenery; his ability to plan and work to a definite budget forms the basis for his practical worth.

The stage and the technician

The scene designer should study the limitations of his stage and should be well equipped to act as his own technician, especially in cases where he must build his own scenery instead of depending upon a technical assistant for the supervision of such work. He should know the width and depth of the stage, the height of the proscenium arch, and any peculiarities of the relationship between the stage and the auditorium, such as their proximity, their shape, the height of balco-

◀ *Design for* The Last of the Lowries,
◀ *by Paul Green. This illustrates the*
◀ *use of a box-setting for a small stage.*
◀ *Designed by Frederick Stover.*

nies, the number and location of galleries, et cetera. The scale of scenic units should correspond to the size of the stage. Scenery for small stages should be small and simple, whereas, for a large stage, scenery is purposely made large and exaggerated in proportion to the scale of the stage. The designer should have a "feeling" for his theatre so that

— 14 —

A PROCESS FOR SCENE DESIGN

he will create settings that will give the impression of "belonging to the particular stage and designed for the benefit of the audience in that particular auditorium." Thus scenery comes to take on special qualities adapted to the theatre in which it is used.

The stage equipment and materials, both permanent and movable, should be so understood that it will be possible to house and handle the scenery with relative ease. By stage equipment is meant the gridiron, the rigging system (whether it is of the old style rope-line-and-pulley type or a counterweight system), trapped area, storage space (offstage, back of cyclorama, side-stage room, et cetera), outdoor sky equipment (cloth cyclorama, plaster dome, or antiquated backdrop), and any special mechanical equipment for the shifting of scenery (wagon, revolving or elevator stages). He should know the amount and type of permanent stage materials and hardware available, such as rollers for plastic units and other devices peculiar to stage use.

Another limitation, not necessarily of the stage but of circumstances, is that of available manpower. If it is an experimental university or little theatre, the designer should give some thought to the people available for building and handling the scenery. Bulky and heavy scenery requires an adequate stage crew for its handling.

After the style has been determined and the materials and supplies have been noted, it is well to study the natural resources of a locality and select the building materials that are easiest and cheapest to procure. This is especially applicable in the case of selecting lumber and canvas used in flat construction. There are many ways to construct scenery, as well as a great variety of materials to be used. In stage building the designer and technician should use substitutes which cost less than the real article. Fortunately, these are often more effective under stage light. A knowledge of the time required to get materials and supplies from other cities forms a valuable aid to the technician. A scenic problem, from the technical point of view, should be studied with relation to the materials needed and to the best possible substitutes obtainable in that locality.

Scenery must be strong and easy to pack and store, especially if it is scheduled to go on the road. In planning scenery, the designer must consider the contemplated run, the ravages of shipping, and the permanency of the scenery with relation to its use. Every opportunity should be given the technician to use his ingenuity in assisting the designer, for co-operation between designer and technician is essential to any harmonious production.

Costumes and the costumer

Stage costumes, in line, mass, and color, and as a moving theatrical element in colored stage light, form one of the most impor-

◀ Sketch for Act Three, "The Queen's
◀ Chamber," in Swinburne's Chastelard.
◀ Conceived as a unit arrangement by
◀ Frederick Stover.

tant factors in determining the physical size and arrangement and color of stage scenery. Luxurious costumes are generally bulky and necessarily require more space and adequate area for the movement and ease of the actors who wear them. Scenery for such costumes is generally constructed in a substantial way, and details are made more permanent than those in settings for the ordinary type of costumes. In general, the attention of an audience may be directed to the action of the play by the subordination of the color of the setting to that of the costumes. The chromatic relationship existing between these two elements is of primary consideration, especially in such matters as harmony and contrast, or

SCENERY—A MANUAL OF DESIGN

the type of color scheme employed, and a great deal depends upon the deft use of color in the establishment of the emotional keynote of the scene.

If the settings and costumes for a production come within the jurisdiction of one person it is only natural that he will plan a definite relationship between them. In such a case, the designer's work consists simply in co-ordinating the two elements.

◀ *Sketch for "The Tower." Two set pieces with removable panels which, by the addition of a third unit, form different combinations.*

In organizations where the scene designer and the costumer are not the same person, the consideration of costumes and the costumer is necessarily of primary importance. In such a case, these two artists should study their individual problems in an attempt to create, in the finished production, a definite aesthetic relation between the scenery and the costuming.

For some plays, the settings are designed with particular regard to their color and value contrasts to the costumes; for other plays, pleasing harmonies between costumes and scenery are most conducive to the expressiveness of the drama. The ideas and designs of the costumer should be respected as far as possible by the scene designer if he would have a unified aesthetic effect in the pictorial and chromatic elements of a stage setting.

Lighting and the lighting artist

Lighting occupies a place of great prominence in modern stage production and the position of the lighting artist has become one of widely accepted importance; he is slowly being graduated from his former job as "electrician" to that of a creative artist, skilled in the conception and use of light as an intensifying agent to drama. In cases where the lighting expert and the scene designer are not the same, it behooves the scene designer to work harmoniously with the lighting artist, so that he may achieve the most imaginative and satisfactory results in the correct presentation of the actors and the scene. In order to understand the lighting artist in his own terms, it is necessary that the scene designer know the principles of stage lighting. He should have a general understanding of the lighting equipment available in the particular theatre in which he is working. Such knowledge should include lighting instruments, their types, the number available for use, switchboards and devices for the control of light, materials, and accessories. A survey should be made of general lighting facilities, and miscellaneous equipment should be noted. The designer should understand the importance of the lighting crew from the point of view of their adequacy and their ability to operate lights effectively. In general, a consideration of stage lighting and the lighting expert promotes greater effectiveness in scenic presentation and assures the harmonious relationship which should exist among all departments of a producing organization.

A PROCESS FOR SCENE DESIGN
Working Drawings

DRAWINGS for scenic production may be classed under two general headings: those of a technical and those of an aesthetic nature. Technical drawings are those which explain the setting from the standpoint of the stage itself, showing in detail the arrangement of the different stage units with reference to each other, together with construction plans for all parts of the setting, and plans made by the draftsman from the designer's drawings to guide the carpenter and technicians in constructing and assembling the scenery on the stage.

Those drawings which are classified as of an aesthetic nature show the stage setting completely visualized, with setting, actors, properties, and lighting unified into a single dramatic effect as they will appear in actual performance, and viewed, therefore, through the proscenium arch. In brief, technical drawings show details of construction and arrangement from the point of view of the technical craftsman, and aesthetic drawings show the proposed effect of the complete production from the standpoint of the audience. To the builder of houses the technical drawings would be the architect's plan of the house; the aesthetic drawings would be the perspective sketch showing any two sides of the house as it will appear when finished.

This chapter will be divided into two parts, the first dealing with the technical drawings, the second with the aesthetic or perspective drawing. This order is by no means mandatory, for unforeseen circumstances often arise which govern the artistic and technical procedure in a dramatic production. Sometimes it is advisable to follow a different plan. Important factors governing drawings of each type will be considered in an attempt to explain their importance with reference to the completed dramatic production.

Technical Drawings

YOUNG designers sometimes have a tendency to disregard or slight the technical drawings for scenery, believing that the finished sketch is all that is required in the execution of a stage setting. When a setting is poorly constructed or the original ideas miscarry, the designer soon learns that the scenic production really rests more upon carefully detailed technical drawings than upon the "dream picture." The designer should learn to create from a plan and furnish complete technical drawings in their proper order. It is much better to prevent a mistake than to try to correct one after it is made. For this reason the importance of technical drawings cannot be overestimated.

Another important thing for designers to remember is that all working drawings should be made on thin, tough tracing paper with a good black pencil in order that clear sharp blueprints can be made for the technical staff.

— 17 —

SCENERY—A MANUAL OF DESIGN

The floor plan

A floor-plan drawing is made from a station point above the stage floor, as one might see the stage from the gridiron, showing the physical arrangement of the different scenic units. It is drawn flatly, in accordance with any architectural scale (usually one-fourth or one-half inch to the foot), and reveals all openings such as doors, windows, and hallways, and all special features, particularly those of a practical nature, such as stairways, balconies, alcoves, fireplaces, bay windows, et cetera, explaining in each case all details of construction and operations.

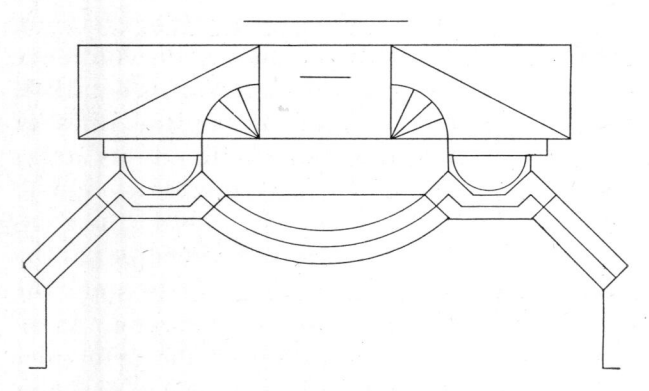

◀ *Floor plan showing arrangement of stage and scenic details (such as step units, platforms, and flats) for a proposed production of Schiller's* Fiasco. *Designed by Harold Helvenston.*

The ingenious arrangement of scenery is important, especially if the play is one of many scenes. The general type and construction of the units, the manner of combining and rearranging them, the general facilities for moving scenery, and the conservation of off-stage space must all be indicated in the designer's floor plan, for it is upon these features that smoothness and rapidity of scene changes depend.

Determine what type of scenery best suits the problem. Is it to be a series of box-settings of flat construction, two-dimensional wings and drops, three-dimensional plastic forms, such as ramps, platforms, et cetera? Or is abstract light to be employed in suggesting most of the scenery? The advantages of two- and three-dimensional scenery should be considered and a decision made as to which is most appropriate to the particular play, production, and stage. There are no infallible rules governing these general types. Actual two-dimensional units may be painted to represent two-dimensional objects—a practice useful in planning sets for musical shows and fantasies. They may be painted in perspective to represent fully visualized landscape or architectural or interior effects, or they may be actually distorted in shape for use in symbolic productions. The artist might, for example, decide to combine flat scenery with fully modeled units in direct relation to their positions on the stage and their proximity to the audience. This problem is one for the director and the designer, and because of its importance, should be primarily treated in the floor plan.

Furniture and important properties should be shown clearly in the floor plan in order that the director may relate the business of the actors to the setting and plan the action in accordance with the actual inclosure with all of its openings and details. The floor plan helps the artist to compose furniture groups in a pleasing manner; it affords an opportunity for the technician to eliminate the building of certain parts of the setting, especially in case furniture is placed against a wall in such a way that the wall is completely shut off from the view of the audience. Architectural detail affects the floor plan only in so far as the placing and arrangement of columns, stairs, platforms, and such details are concerned.

In the floor plan, the artist is able to assist the lighting expert or electrician by showing actual positions in which lighting instruments may be placed in order to afford the unobstructed use of light upon a setting. A floor plan is invaluable to the lighting expert for studying his problem with a view to special features of the setting, such as the depth of the back wall, the openings to be used for the suggestions of exterior effects, the use of vertical light stands or towers, and the attachment of special lighting equipment actually upon scenic units.

If the designer does not wish to spend time in drawing the entire plan to scale, he may use graph paper, its uniform rulings elim-

SCENE DESIGN—WORKING DRAWINGS

inating the need of an architect's scale. Floor plans are ordinarily made in pencil; however, it is extremely helpful in the understanding of a floor plan to outline the basic contours of the setting with a wash line. This readily assists the observer in understanding the definite shape of a setting.

For the convenience of both director and artist, a number of different proposed floor plans are generally made of each setting used in a production. These drawings, showing the various ways in which a setting can be physically arranged, are given the director, who chooses the one which suits him best, from the points of view of its peculiar adaptability to his action, its suitability to the play, and its own intrinsic charm. The designer should always be willing to assist the director in the making of any number of sketches and to persevere in this process until an ideal plan is conceived.

The floor plan suggests its own importance in that from it all other drawings are developed. For this reason, the designer should exert his best energies in devising a good plan. Adaptability of the settings to the action the director has planned, possibilities for the designer's own aesthetic treatment of the setting, economy in the building cost as well as economy in the use of scenic units, and methods of the facile handling of scenery all share equally in determining a good floor plan.

The size of the stage floor, the height of the proscenium arch, the height and slope of the orchestra, balcony, and galleries, and the shape and size of the auditorium as well as the general relationship of the latter to the stage—all impose special conditions in regard to size and arrangement of scenery on the stage. Scenery should always be designed in scale to the size of the stage in its relation to the auditorium.

An extremely important point which may well be brought up here is the influence which the size of the theatre and its physical limitations will exert upon the arrangement of the scenic units on the stage. For example, if the auditorium is fan-shaped and a perfectly square setting is used, it is obvious that the section of the audience sitting on one extreme side of the auditorium might miss seeing the action if it took place on the same side of the stage—especially in the upstage areas. By the same token, if the setting is too low, people sitting high in the balcony might not be able to see a chandelier hanging from the ceiling. In both cases, the size and shape of the stage floor, the height of the proscenium arch, the height and slope of orchestra, balcony, and gallery, and the general shape and size of the auditorium must be taken into consideration in order that the greatest part of the audience shall see all of the important action of the play. It is obviously the consideration, then, of sight lines that should govern the designer in planning his settings with reference to the physical layout of the theatre.

Literally, sight lines are the lines of vision between the eyes of anyone in the audience and the stage setting, inclusive of its detail. It is important to include within the lines of vision the complete stage with all its areas and objects. The designer should attempt to design settings which can be seen in their entirety by the greatest number of people; at the same time, of course, trying not to spoil the aesthetic effect and scale of the scene. As an example of the application of the principles of the use of sight lines, suppose a designer wishes to represent a normally realistic room on the stage. If the particular theatre is built so that the stage is merely one end of a long auditorium, such a room can be arranged in realistic fashion with all of its walls at right angles to each other, the designer knowing that the stage setting in its entirety comes within the vision of everyone in the audience. However, if the auditorium is fan-shaped the physical setting may be modified in shape so as to afford almost every one in the audience a complete view. The side walls of such a setting would necessarily have to be raked or drawn in diagonally from the tormentors or sides of the proscenium toward the area center back. Such an arrangement would cause the setting to converge slightly toward the center of the upstage area. In such cases the degree of convergence is determined by the shape and size of the auditorium in its relationship to the stage.

In the case of theatres with balconies, sight lines affect the height of the teaser also.

SCENERY—A MANUAL OF DESIGN

From the high seats in the balcony and galleries, it is often impossible for spectators to see much of the rear area of the settings. Full view of the actors and the important pictorial and acting areas of the setting should be worked out by the designer. A compromise is often attempted, and balcony spectators are allowed to see a greater part of the action but not all of it. A designer, by the use of scaled floor plans and sectional diagrams of the theatre, is able to draw lines between the extreme points of vision and the stage, and thus determine the width and shape of the stage and setting and the height of the scenic units and the teaser. The amount of attention a designer pays to sight lines becomes quite evident later on in the perspective sketch.

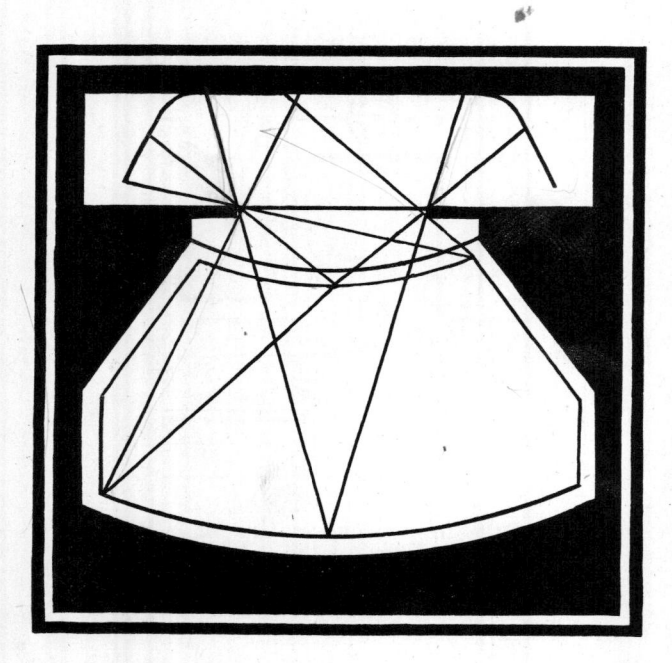

◀ *Drawing to show application of the theory of sight lines, in a plan of auditorium and stage.*

Elevations

An elevation is a detailed drawing of any single vertical plane within a stage setting, and is generally developed from the perspective sketch of the designer. For the reason that it follows the perspective sketch, it might seem that it would actually follow the latter in the treatment of scenic drawings; however, because an elevation is drawn flatly to scale, it becomes, more than anything, a mechanical drawing and, as such, I prefer to deal with it here.

The elevation drawing serves both the designer and the technician. By the preparation of such a drawing, the designer analyzes his own pictorial sketch in complete detail, learning, as it were, the physical necessities of the actual setting. Details barely suggested in the perspective sketch assume definite size and shape in the elevation. Furniture is explained in detailed relation to the walls and properties; the aesthetic effect of each main area should be determined by means of an elevation. Architectural detail is explained thoroughly in the elevation; the demands of the designer are rendered clear in graphic form. It is at this stage of scene design that a great many problems are solved regarding the prac-

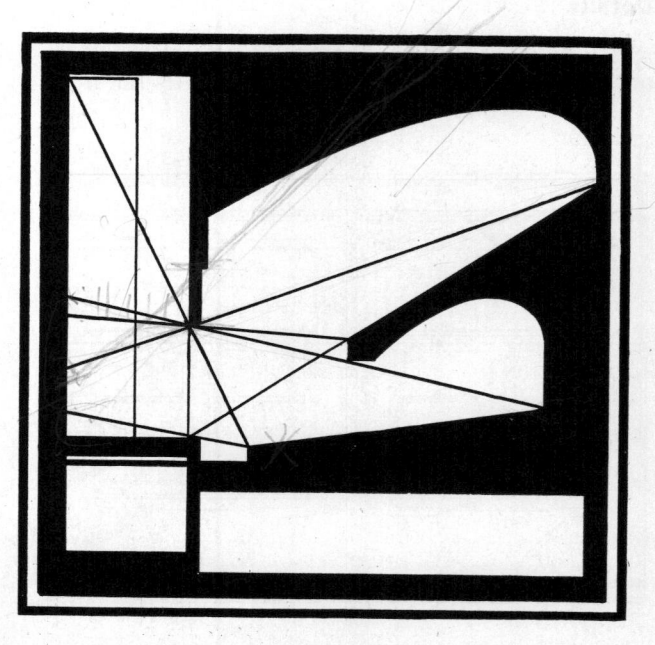

◀ *Sectional view of auditorium and stage. Note the sight lines from the balcony.*

ticability of details such as cornices, mouldings, baseboards, dadoes, paneling, et cetera. The questions to be settled are generally affected by the personal whims of the designer

SCENE DESIGN—WORKING DRAWINGS

and his ability to compromise successfully with the technician, the latter generally approaching the problem from the point of view of economy of building costs and manual labor.

Elevations are made for the technician, who is called upon to construct actual scenery from the settings as drawn. The technician turns the elevations over to the draftsman, who prepares drawings showing the rear side of each detail. Such a drawing guides the carpenters in the exact backstage construction of each unit of scenery. From such working drawings the technician is able to estimate the cost of the scenery and the amount of materials necessary for its construction.

This type of drawing is invaluable to the technical production department, and a scene designer is not considered completely competent until he is able to prepare such drawings from the sketches of completely visualized settings.

Details

In a great many cases detailed drawings are necessary for certain special units such as

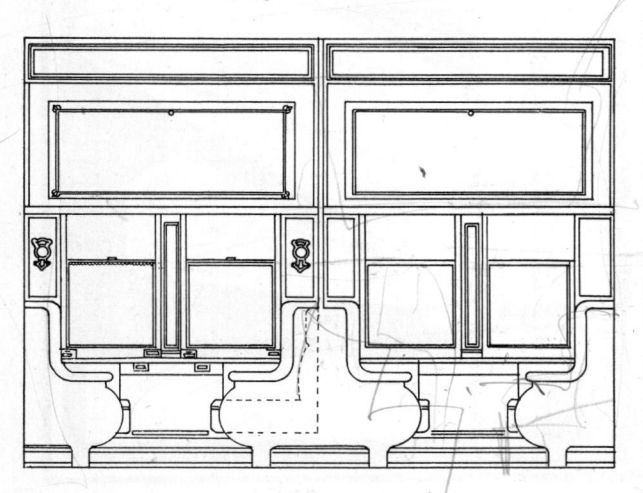

◀ *Drawing of an elevation showing details of a Pullman car setting. This is a measured drawing from actual observation by Harold Helvenston.*

fireplaces, bay windows, seats in railway coaches, ceilings, pieces of furniture, and other large properties. These can be drawn in isometric fashion with complete disregard for perspective principles, or they may be drawn in the form of separate elevations for each plane of a scenic unit.

Detailed drawings are usually made to a much larger scale than elevations, so that

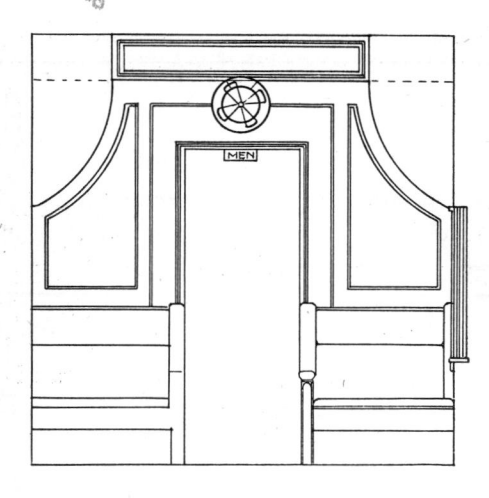

◀ *Drawing of a cross-section of a Pullman car setting showing doorway; exactly to scale.*

minute parts can be readily understood by the builder. In some cases, a larger scale allows for the artist's expression of some object which he has indicated in an indefinite or casual way in his perspective sketch. This form of drawing is indispensable in the workshop and serves as a definite guide to the workman. There is nothing so disheartening to both artist and technician as to learn that, by carelessness or negligence in planning scenery, a unit has been either constructed in a poor manner or made larger or smaller than originally intended by the artist. It is of great benefit to the artist to see that the technician, the draftsman, and the builder are supplied with such details if he would have his designs executed with accuracy and with the charm of his original conception. A detail is the more particularly described unit of the whole, and its use assures the greatest degree of accuracy in the execution of stage scenery.

Cross-sections

Sometimes there is need for a fourth kind of drawing, called a cross-section or section.

SCENERY—A MANUAL OF DESIGN

This sort of drawing generally shows a view along a wall or looking down upon a certain piece of stagecraft in order that a correct relation may be understood and maintained between two or three different units which are to be used together. Doorways, windows, and other such units are sometimes drawn in this manner; however, this is often left to the draftsman or the technician to solve and to render into readable drawings.

The Scenic Sketch

THE DESIGNER, in the preliminary considerations of a dramatic production, thinks of scenery in relation to the following: the play and its general form, the particular theatre in which it is to be produced — its stage and auditorium, and the adherence of the settings to the chosen style of production with a view to their aesthetic combination with costumes and light. From such considerations, he prepares the floor plan, a mechanical drawing. He then turns to his own particular function in the art of scene design — that of making the graphic representation or the drawing of the setting, with an eye toward properties, costumes, and light, fully visualized through the proscenium arch. Such a drawing is called a perspective sketch. In this type of drawing, the designer departs from the technical elements of the scene and works to refine and develop an artistic theme according to his own distinctive and individual sense of beauty. This form of drawing is made from the floor plan agreed upon by the director. It is well to select a definite scale, usually one-half inch to the foot, drawing the proscenium arch to scale and projecting the actual setting behind the opening following the principles of one- or two-point perspective, the former being more commonly used than the latter. It is always best to make an accurate perspective drawing which can later be modified to suit the aesthetic sense of the artist. Definite station-points, horizon lines, vanishing- and measuring-points, determined by means of the scaled floor plan, should be employed in the preparation of such a sketch. All furnishings and other objects should be drawn as accurately as possible in the preliminary planning of an aesthetic representation; the designer should remember that the use of line, coupled with light, produces mass formations which go toward making the sketch dramatic in effect.

The drawing of the scenic sketch is generally the most delightful part of the artistic process. The designer's personal ideas combine with the known elements of the play in the creation of an atmospheric background for the action thereof. He becomes his own master.

Simplified realistic setting for Ibsen's Brand. Designed by Harold Helvenston. This would require a large stage, as indicated by the size of the figures.

The great inspiration

In nearly every production the artist at some time or other gets a "big idea" which sets him off to a good start. This big idea may take the form of a special plan for handling the scenery; it may suggest itself in an unusual composition in line, color, or light effects; or it may offer an interesting emphasis of a special phase of scenery, any form of which, developed in his designs for the set-

SCENE DESIGN—WORKING DRAWINGS

tings, becomes his own personal creation and elevates him to the position of artist. The big idea usually comes like a whirlwind out of a clear sky; it is born of an "original impulse" —it takes concrete form and lives and, in some instances, grows to the stature of an obsession. These are the most precious moments to the artist, for at this time nothing else in the world around him matters; he forgets all in quest of his goal, in search for the best solution to his problem and the fulfillment of an idea. This is the truly creative stage of scene design and the time when unusual conceptions are born. Such an "original impulse" should be followed as closely as possible in conceiving scenic ideas, for it is the all-important element upon which rest the strength, the beauty, and the charm of an artistic scenic production. An artist's first ideas are very valuable, and when these ideas come notes should be made, rough sketches drawn, and these as fast as they come to mind; for sometimes, in the hurried mental shuffle, ideas are lost or forgotten. The greater the number of basic ideas an artist has to begin with, the better chance he has to select an unusual one. The first ideas of an original scene generally come in the form of visual patterns as viewed through the proscenium arch. Floor plans may be temporarily forgotten when these compositions come to mind. They generally apply to the dramatic production as a whole; however, special scenes suggest themselves, sometimes with extraordinary vividness.

This type of special conception sometimes comes before the floor plan is made; again it may come during the process of drawing the perspective sketch; and in some instances it develops even after all the settings have been drawn, and after the actual work on the production has been started. The proper time for such ideas, however, is just before the perspective sketch is made, so that the artistic conception can be rendered in graphic form, and detailed drawings of the special effects can be made. The perspective sketch is extremely important because it is the starting-point for elevations and details, as well as the guide for the ensemble effect of the different elements in visual stage production.

Elements of the perspective sketch

There are a number of very important factors that enter into the drawing of a perspective sketch, and the degree of accuracy with which the sketch may be used as an actual guide to scenic production is directly proportional to the manner in which the designer has definitely represented such factors. These factors include: size and proportion of the stage, the requirements of the particular theatre as to sight lines, the color of the setting with relation to the atmosphere of the play, and the effect of stage light upon the color, the suggestion of architecture and furniture necessary in setting, the representation of the size of the setting by the use of scaled objects, and the extent to which a scene designer desires to commit himself in the drawing. The amount of attention that a designer pays to these factors determines greatly the success of his general ability as a scene designer and often governs the ease with which the production staff is able to secure the effects desired by the director and the designer.

The size and proportion of the permanent proscenium opening is generally carried out or suggested in the sketch; however, just as it is possible for these conditions to be modified by the rearrangement and readjustment of the tormentors and the teaser, it is easy for the designer to suggest such special modification in his actual sketch. It is common for a designer to suggest a lower teaser for an interior setting than he does for one of exterior character. The element of a low ceiling assists in suggesting the closed-in aspect of a room, while an abundance of space above the ground and the objects in an exterior setting helps to emphasize the illusion of sky and the out-of-doors.

Despite the fact that the perspective sketch is conceived from one definite station-point in the auditorium, the designer usually suggests, in his sketch, the maximum range of vision afforded from any place in the auditorium. From the floor plan he is able to determine accurately the visual limitations resulting from the sight lines. The degree of precision with which he may suggest the general view of a stage setting through the proscenium arch depends upon his station-point;

SCENERY—A MANUAL OF DESIGN

◀ *Setting for Stanford University production of Čapek's* The Makropolous Secret. *This photograph shows how every detail of the setting is co-ordinated in rhythmic design. All furniture and properties were designed especially for the setting by Harold Helvenston.*

if the drawing is made from one side of the house, it is natural that the sketch will reveal more of the opposite side of the stage, and the nearest wall to the observer will be less open to view than the farthest wall. The same generalization may be made about the height of the station-point employed by the designer. From a station-point in the orchestra, one is able to see more of the ceiling and less of the floor, and, by reverse token, from the balcony one perceives more of the floor than of the ceiling. In any event, the designer in his sketch should present an adequate view of the stage, in its entirety, to the greatest number of the people in the audience, both from the orchestra and from the balconies and galleries. The perspective sketch, more than any other type of scenic drawing, should approximate an idea of the stage setting as viewed by the audience; thus, sight lines and their adjustment, represented in the visual sketch of a setting, become an item of extreme importance.

In stage settings and in stage drawings, color and light must be inseparable in the designer's mind; it is imperative that color, on the stage, be thought of in terms of pigment plus colored light. Since the element of light in stage drawings is of such tremendous importance, the designer should conceive a theory of lighting based upon an emotional and aesthetic conception of the play in hand. He must use his knowledge of the physical laws and the natural qualities of stage light in arriving at such a conception. He should plan his lighting first, conceiving it in its own natural quality or using it unrealistically as a means to abstraction.

An approximate effect of actual lighting can always be shown in the sketch. Certain objects merge into others and sometimes certain units of the setting merge into darkness. Sharp lines, often offensive to the eye, should be softened for stage drawings unless the designer purposely wishes to use such lines in emphasis of a dramatic or artistic value in the setting. The suggestion of light in terms of intensity can be successfully employed to create, in the stage drawing, definite patterns in light and shade; the intrinsic color of the light at the same time may be used to suggest special emotional effects. The quality of light in a stage sketch often assists the lighting expert in approximating the same effect in actual stage production. The flexibilities, limitations, and uses of light form a valuable study for the designer. It is by the use of line, mass, and light that a designer creates visual

SCENE DESIGN—WORKING DRAWINGS

pattern in light and shade. Such a pattern can, with sufficient study, be accurately suggested in a stage sketch.

In the drawing and rendering of stage designs, architectural subjects form a definite problem; the designer should know just how faithfully he should represent anything as definite as architecture. There is no special rule about architectural representation in scene sketches, and a great deal depends upon lighting. If the lighting comes from behind an arcade, then it is easy to see that the structure itself becomes a silhouette and can be represented as such in a drawing. If the light is directed from the front of the stage back upon an architectural façade, then it is obvious that more detail and graphic explanation is necessary in the sketch. It is usually a good plan to draw architectural details and units carefully in pencil in the original and then to try to attain a certain air of indefiniteness or mystery in the rendering of them. In this way we have a scientific foundation upon which is based an artistic rendering. This rule holds good for a great many details of scenic rendition. The governing aesthetic idea of the play and its manner of production, and the artistic sense of the designer all enter in to create, not architectural subjects, but the simple spirit of them in the scene sketch as well as in the actual setting.

Furniture can be employed as definitely as any other element to assist in building a visual pattern in the stage setting, and for this reason its representation in the perspective sketch is important. In contrast to the moving actor, furniture remains stationary as an element of decoration and, on account of this fact, should be pleasingly related to the various acting areas and the many details of the setting. Balance and harmony in a stage setting are gained by the combination of moving actors and static furniture into definite shapes and pictorial effects. Stage directions and the physical limitations of a stage might cause the director to use furniture in an exaggerated or unrealistic manner; however, the designer should always be able to combine furniture into interesting groups. Generally speaking, certain pieces of furniture are planned as the dominant spots in a stage setting in accordance with their use and their association with actors in person; again special articles of furniture may simply contribute to the setting by their pleasing arrangement or grouping; and at other times a setting is made conspicuously

◀ *A scene from the Chinese play* Peking Politics. *In this setting it is easy to determine the scale of every object in the room. The furniture was decorated by papier-mâché ornament. Designed by Harold Helvenston.*

SCENERY—A MANUAL OF DESIGN

interesting by the very absence of furniture. No other element can make a stage sketch seem as incomplete or as amateurishly and carelessly designed as the inartistic use and the poor drawing of furniture. However, in scene sketches, the designer is allowed a certain amount of liberty. He might suggest furniture in a very slight manner in one setting, the subtlety of his drawing depending either upon the degree of his accurate knowledge of the furniture or upon his uncertainty as to the selection of pieces; or, again, he might represent each piece of furniture in portrait form, showing every detail. The manner of drawing and representing furniture in a perspective drawing depends upon the stylistic traits of the artist, the importance of the piece of furniture, and the mood intended in the drawing.

The scale of a stage setting is important and should be understood through the scene design, because it provides a method for judging the dimensions and the relative sizes of scenic details and units by comparison with familiar objects. For instance, one might observe the sketch of a setting without having any idea as to the dimensions of picturized detail, but when a man, a chair, or an object of known size is added, the scale is established and the dimensions of the setting can be mentally approximated. The human figure serves as the readiest means of giving scale to a setting, especially in so far as the introduction of it into a sketch allows the observer to determine the relationship between the actors and the scenery.

Media and rendering

Any medium can be employed by the designer in the rendering of a perspective drawing for the stage; however, the media used most frequently are pencil, pen and ink, ink and wash, charcoal, water color (both transparent and opaque), oil color, and lithographic pencil. There are various ways by which essentially different media may be combined to produce unusual artistic effects. Such combinations as charcoal and water color, pencil and water color, pen and ink and color, and pastel chalks on gray paper are often used by designers in the drawing of perspective sketches. Often a designer becomes known by the combination of media which he uses. In general, it matters little what medium is used in the making of a stage sketch, as long as the results are dramatic in visual effect. It remains for each

◀ *Stage setting from* Peking Politics, *showing the effectiveness of simplicity in stage design. The window up center was made of translucent silk; the design was painted with show-card color and lighted from the rear; hence the mellow glow. Settings by Harold Helvenston.*

— 26 —

SCENE DESIGN—WORKING DRAWINGS

Another setting from Peking Politics *exhibiting the same quality of simplicity in design. Splendid draperies were made by stenciling a brilliant yellow material with silver. In this setting the furniture was specially designed for the play.*

individual designer to experiment with the various media which best express his personality in stage sketches.

Aesthetic qualities of the sketch

The same qualities that characterize a fine stage setting should be represented in a drawing for the theatre. They are: strength and simplicity of line, dynamic and toned color, a feeling of action, a fine sense of imagination resulting in subtle exaggeration and loftiness, a feeling for the use of stage light to create an air of mystery or suggestion—all these combined into an impelling unit of dramatic background for the living representation of the actor. Some of these elements may be found, amplified to the point of greatness, in the paintings of artists not of the theatre. One does well, therefore, to regard the work of eminent artists as sources for the study of these dominant qualities. The point to be enforced is that the stage drawing must have something of them all in order to express the special quality that is, in itself, akin to the theatre.

The fairy tale illustrations of Edmund Dulac and Arthur Rackham illustrate a special type of coloration. In these, the detail, as well as the color, constitutes part of their quaint charm; and added to these factors, there is always a fine imaginative quality in their drawings. This quality finds an easy place in stage sketches for fantastic plays or children's drama.

Then comes the all-important quality of light in drawings—shades of Rembrandt! Observe his "Presentation in the Temple" and realize how truly great light can be in a composition. See how, even in a certain arbitrary fashion, he has woven light into his design in quest of emphasis. People weave into a pattern. Scenery becomes mystic suggestion, and costumes colored symbols of an idea. And all this is bathed with light. Rembrandt's pictures, as a whole, are glorious expressions in light. Its importance and its power are not to be denied. Rembrandt recognized it as a medium, mastered it, and exploited it.

Take Winslow Homer's painting, "The Gulf Stream," depicting the Caribbean Sea after a storm. The tiny boat is a hopeless wreck, drifting helplessly in a trough of the sea; the frightened negro lying flat across the boat contemplating the sharks. What an emotion comes from a little creation of paint! An atmosphere of calm and a feeling of the

— 27 —

SCENERY—A MANUAL OF DESIGN

fury of the storm are the results, and a picture has caused it all! Now transplant that quality into a stage drawing by the sheer placid quality of the painting. The very essence of a scene can be suggested, and an artist can cause the observer to experience the thrill that comes from having lived through a tropical storm.

Simplicity of line is one of the essential characteristics of good stage sketches. The works of Hendrik Van Loon, Covarrubias, and George Bellows here come to mind. In their drawings this quality is found in an exaggerated form. The directness of their intention and the charm of their drawings lie in this beautiful simplicity. Other qualities of importance are also found in their stage drawings. In Van Loon's sketches, he brings about an emphasis of his subject by economy of detail. A bridge is a bridge and nothing else. Unnecessary detail is left out of his compositions, and the subject treated is not subordinated by the intrusion of trivial objects. Such economy of detail should be a feature of drawings for the stage—it is in keeping with the directness of drama, and is to be desired in any form of dramatic expression. Covarrubias illustrates the quality of simple exaggeration that is very necessary in stage drawing. As the result of a highly developed selection of line, his works reveal a rare insight into the subject treated. George Bellows' lithographs show the value of using simple line and technique to create power and vigor in drawings. None of his figures sleep—even in the dead as he conceives them there is a feeling of power. Stage drawings should possess this same quality in order to express the dramatic finality of the play.

The coloring of a stage drawing should be unusual. The selection of hues and the composition of hues and values should result from a process of careful thought; each integral area of color within the plane of the sketch should be related to the other, and all of them to the whole. In order to realize the charm of exquisitely toned color, look at a painting of Jules Guérin, at Japanese prints, at one of Frank Brangwyn's bridge sketches, at a painting by Zuloaga, or even at an etching by Anders Zorn. Each of these is different in coloration and technique, and yet all of them possess the rare quality of tone which results in a rich feeling of power.

Guérin's renderings of architectural subjects are perfect examples of toned harmonies which, in their skilful execution, serve to emphasize the subtle contrasts in his pictures. Take his painting of "The Alamo" for example: here we see a mission type of stronghold, powerful in its compositional loneliness, and serene in the tranquillity of a southern night. Tiny figures imprisoned in shadow give it scale. There is a chromatic sympathy existing between these figures, the gaunt building, and the night itself, and even in their diminutive size they create a feeling of strength. The color is quiet and deeply subtle.

Aside from the deft handling of line in Japanese prints, we find almost invariably an underlying soft tone of color. This quality fuses the objects into a harmonious picture, illustrating again the importance of tone.

Look at an etching by Anders Zorn. Subtle delineation and vague vignette combine with monochromatic tone to give it unity. The grayness or tone of the print relieves the otherwise obvious feeling of a line drawing. This quality of tonality in stage sketches, as well as in actual settings, is essential, especially in so far as the consciousness of make-believe and the obviousness of materials affect one's sense of values. In almost every drawing and setting for the theatre, there is an excuse for tonality, and in most cases it is essentially a factor which can go to make it delightful to look at and unobtrusive as a background for actors.

Brangwyn, in his use of color, gives a definite sense of tone, perhaps more vigorous than Guérin's, but none the less effective. At will he conjures up the spirit of age with color and of strength with line. His things are done with great freedom and with the spirit of an artist who knows when to stop.

Again, color may be used to create a feeling of action. For this type of coloration, one's mind goes to the painting of a dancing girl or a toreador by Zuloaga. In his paintings there is a disregard for small detail, and in his courageous handling of a bit of dashing color in a costume one feels the very movements of

— 28 —

SCENE DESIGN—WORKING DRAWINGS

the figure, the swishing of a skirt, the whirling of a cape! The color is sweeping and full of passion. The backgrounds of these paintings are in simple idealized colors—the human figures themselves become the spirit of Spain— a patch of brilliant red their passion and glory. The focal point of Zuloaga's paintings is definitely gained by the skilful use of brilliant color and as studies in art they serve to illustrate the idealized effect of figures arranged in group formation—a quality which the scene designer should understand and should incorporate in his drawing.

Henry Raleigh in his exquisite drawings suggests a feeling of loftiness, open air, and space. In his faces there is a certain wistfulness that elevates the observer to higher planes. His sketches are idealizations of things already beautiful and, as intrinsically illustrative, cause one to want to read the story accompanying them. In the dreaminess of a person's eyes and the tilt of a girl's head, one senses a quality the artist would like to find in reality but seldom does. Feel the pleasure of this artist as his pencil searches for these imaginative, wistful postures. Look at the pond with lilies in it and you are looking into the soul of the girl and boy in the canoe above it. Each thing in the picture seems to soar away into mystery. Then—back to the theatre with its settings and sketches! Why should they not go up into the sky! Why does it matter where the top is, so long as there is one! Who has a more perfect opportunity to use this sense of loftiness than an artist who designs stage settings?

Noncommittal qualities of the sketch

One of the principal factors that go to make stage work fascinating is the very mystery of its atmosphere. Obvious in its qualities of deception, it offers a splendid chance to the designer for the suggestion of this mystery and for pleasing artificiality in his sketches. The representation of light offers a natural reason for the more or less noncommittal qualities in a stage sketch; however, the use of such quality lies within the province of the designer—in his intention and purpose in such representation. The designer almost always has some purpose in mind, either direct or indirect, and its quality is seldom just a mere accident in his rendering.

It is sometimes necessary to give only the general effect in the sketch with little attention to clearly defined detail. In this way the designer is allowed the liberty to develop or to modify details during the course of construction and painting of the setting, and this without the loss of dignity attendant upon denying a previously made graphic statement. In making the sketch, perseverance in getting the desired results is a necessary attribute of the designer, and if he is sincere in his work he is not content with his idea or sketch until he has made it as flawless as he can, even though the director has signified his approval before that degree of perfection is reached.

From another point of view, a designer might be working in a locality where facilities for getting special properties are extremely limited; then it would seem perfectly natural for him to indicate in the sketch the general types of furniture and properties, depending, as it were, upon a close approximation of these in the actual setting. In many instances there is the possibility of using any of a variety of properties, each of them of the same general decorative feeling, yet each somewhat different from the others in its special details. The designer sometimes takes the liberty of indicating the general type of object without committing himself as to its detail, knowing that any object of the general type can be used with equal accuracy and imagination. In such use, the noncommittal quality is not essentially a form of "artistic hedging," though it is possible for a careless or neglectful designer to take unfair advantage of such a quality, otherwise charming in legitimate use. He can be noncommittal for the purpose of masking his ignorance about period design and architectural forms, just as bad drawings are passed off upon the public under the guise of modern art. The use of this noncommittal quality as a device, and the effectiveness of it, is directly proportional to the type of production, the financial status of the producing company, the limitations of the locality in which a play is being produced, and the knowledge of the designer and his

SCENERY—A MANUAL OF DESIGN

◀ *Scene sketch for setting used in the Stanford University production*
◀ *of Ibsen's* The Wild Duck. *In this wash drawing light and shadows*
◀ *play a major part in revealing the mood of the drama.*

ability not only to represent an idea faithfully but to endeavor to execute a design with reasonable accuracy. This quality is used to different degrees by different designers and, in general, is pleasing. However, a designer must consider many factors in determining the degree to which he will employ such practice, realizing the requirements of a visual sketch as being the most truthful pictorial idea of the setting to be had before the actual production, and knowing that almost any perspective sketch requires elevations and details in explanation of its own peculiar features and special physical character.

The artist's style

By the skilful use of a medium, an artist of the theatre can combine in his drawings a number of these qualities. By his technique in the use of line and color and light he can

◀ *Photograph of actual setting made from the sketch above. This il-*
◀ *lustrates the evolution of a setting from the sketch. The production*
◀ *was directed by Gordon Davis and designed by Harold Helvenston.*

— 30 —

SCENE DESIGN—WORKING DRAWINGS

command the emotions of the observer—the audience. Sun, wind, and rain can pour out of his drawings; human beings can become abstract in mass; horror can skulk in every detail of a sketch for a tragedy; and, likewise, a drawing can laugh its way into comedy by the use of warmth and light. Colors become people and people become colors; color can tone the audience into emotion and perhaps, above all these qualities, the sketch will have that intangible, fine sense of action so necessary in the theatre.

The combination of such rare qualities in

◂ *Sketch for ship setting in* Tristan and Isolde. *An example of sweeping line in a stage setting. Designed by Harold Helvenston.*

drawings marks the artist and proclaims his style. I do not mean to say that all stage designs should possess all of these qualities or even almost all of them. I simply mean that a drawing for the theatre should, as much as possible, go out of the realm of normal illustration and decorative painting and become something having dynamic force within the theatre.

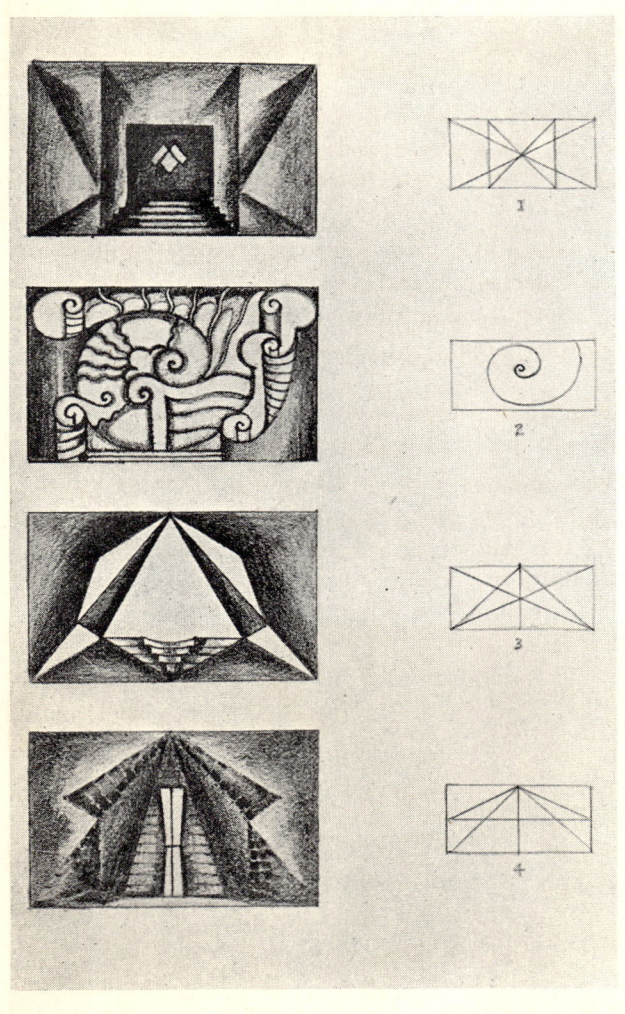

After having learned to define these qualities by studying the work of other types of artists, one should look open-eyed into the drawings made for the theatre and try to find in them as many of these subtleties as possible. If one can remember that simplicity is aesthetically synonymous with beauty, that color is the keynote to emotion, that well-directed exaggeration is a virtue of the theatre; if one will keep in mind the loveliness of sweeping spaces and the emphasis that comes with a deft bit of lighting—he will begin to realize not only the qualities that make a good theatrical sketch but the finest attributes of a good stage setting.

◂ *Sketches showing the evolution of stage settings along definite basic lines. From the author's sketchbook.*

A PROCESS FOR SCENE DESIGN
The Scene Model

IT is often advisable to prepare scaled models of stage settings in preference to visual sketches, or, in some cases, to use models as explanations of stage sketches—not only for greater clearness for the designer himself but also for assisting better the director and the actor. Scene models possess several marked advantages.

A three-dimensional model affords the director an opportunity to study the scene from every conceivable angle and to envisage the action of the play within its physical setting. Through its use, acting areas may be studied in their proper proportions and relationships. In many instances difficult problems of action and business can be solved more quickly and easily by using a model than by the trial-and-error method of the more or less indefinite stage sketch. Models are of special value to the director in his consideration of plastic or constructivist settings.

A scene model, moreover, affords the actor an excellent opportunity to feel out his stage action, to anticipate and correct possible difficulties in the use of the real setting, and to become accustomed to its special physical arrangements. A plastic model is of great benefit to the actor in such settings as rocky exteriors, Indian pueblos, or scenes requiring an irregular ground formation. It promotes a clearer understanding of acting areas and levels, their relationships, entrances and exits, and practical details peculiar to this particular type of stage setting.

For the artist, a scene model is invaluable. By its use he is able to visualize the complete setting and can more easily determine the final arrangement of each detail, area, and elevation. In a model he commits himself more thoroughly than he generally does in a perspective sketch; corners and jogs become definite, and the sizes and shapes of details are explained in three dimensions. The suggestion of detail in his sketch assumes concrete proportion in his model. The manner of construction and the type of actual building materials are implied to a greater degree in model form than in the usual sketch for a setting. By placing the model setting in a miniature theatre or model-box, the designer is able to view the model from every angle through the proscenium arch, thereby getting the point of view of the audience from any position in the house; whereas, in the perspective sketch, the scene is drawn from one particular point within the house and the other views can be only mentally approximated.

A scene model offers complete opportunity to the artist for the juxtaposition of units and the flexible possibilities of a setting, especially in the case of planning semi-permanent settings. Another feature of the models is that the artist is able to experiment with paint on the setting, and with the effects of stage lighting on the pigment. In short, the model affords the designer a complete chance to study not only the physical scenery for a play but also the aesthetic effects to be gained by the combination of paint and light and moving actors. By working it out in detailed form the artist knows that the setting will fit the stage and that as a means of assisting the play's action it will please the director; he also knows that it will afford the

SCENE DESIGN—THE MODEL

actor an advance opportunity to capitalize the features of the setting.

Although the type of scene model which I have been discussing is valuable pre-eminently in the case of irregular settings, it is not to be disregarded as a helpful device in preparing even the simplest box setting. In the planning of settings for operas and operettas and other types of musical shows, the model forms a more definite starting-point than the sketch; the artist there commits himself as to size, shape, detail, and arrangement on the stage.

It is debatable whether or not the painting of the miniature stage setting is of very great assistance to the scene-painter. Painted detail is necessarily represented on so small a scale that at most the colors can only roughly approximate the actual color to be used on the real setting. It often happens that radical changes have to be made in the painting of the full-sized setting. In general, the painting of stage models offers merely an idea of the color desired by the designer.

It is often advisable to make rough sketches of a scene and from these to construct rough models in order that the most pleasing and practicable one may be selected by the director for final detailed execution. This is especially true in the case of a plastic or a semi-permanent setting. Beeswax or soap forms an excellent substance for making very small sketch models of a plastic setting. Razor blades and knives can be used to model the structural units.

◀ *Photograph of model made from preceding sketch. This illustrates the accuracy possible in the execution of a stage model from the original sketch.*

For all practical purposes in using a scene model it is best to have a model theatre scaled to the actual theater to be used. This affords an excellent chance to study the complete project. If, however, the model proscenium is too large, its teaser can be lowered and its tormentors pulled on stage to approximate the size and effect of the theatre in question. If this is impractical, an ordinary box should be constructed and fitted with a proscenium and stage corresponding in size and proportion to those of the real theatre. In any event, the model stage or model-box should be of the same scale as the scene model. It is very difficult to display properly a one-fourth-inch-scale model in a one-half-inch-scale theatre, especially if the model lighting instruments correspond to the scale of the latter. In the more elaborate model stages, such fittings as draw curtains, trapped doors, complete gridiron with flylines, and model lighting system can be installed; the conveniences of the actual stage may be used even in model form.

In building a scene model, it is usually best to construct it to the scale of one-half inch to the foot, this particular scale being commonly accepted as standard by the majority of designers. The one-fourth-inch scale is sometimes satisfactory; however, with the larger scale details become more definite and the finished model is executed with more finesse. Sometimes in the hazy and diminutive one-fourth-inch-scale model the setting is in itself charming but in the actual execution of the setting from the model these details count for little and the designer has to re-

◀ *Sketch for the Epilogue to Shaw's Saint Joan, as conceived by Alma Steininger. The drawing was made in pencil, the highlights with an eraser.*

SCENERY—A MANUAL OF DESIGN

◀ *A cardboard model setting for* The Rendezvous of the Unknown Soldier, *written by Maurice Gnesin, and designed by Harold Helvenston.*

adjust, revise, or completely re-design the entire setting. It is much better to assure accuracy in the actual execution of a scene by constructing the model to a larger scale. One-inch-scale models are sometimes very valuable, although they are hard to render in detail and often prove bulky in handling. However, if the model theatre is of one-half-inch scale, the model setting should correspond. And from the point of view of lighting the model setting, the one-inch scale sometimes corresponds more accurately to the model lighting instruments used, especially in the case of standard equipment.

There is no end to the materials and tools available for use in making scene models; it is for the individual designer to choose his own materials with relation to the special physical and aesthetic qualities needed in the setting. This flexible phase of scene-model technique offers an opportunity for the designer to exploit new substances and to develop any experimental ideas he may have concerning model scenecraft.

In making of models, there is but one general rule to be followed. Just as in the execution of actual scenery, it is a bad policy to construct anything that is unnecessary from the point of view of the actor and director, and anything that is not within view of the audience. It is considered to be "good stagecraft" if all the visual unessentials are left out. In both model and actual construction the observance of this rule cuts the expense of labor and materials and eliminates a great deal of extra personal worry on the part of designer and technician. However, it should be understood that backings for doors, rooms and hallways, stairways, ceilings, and exterior details, visible to the audience in the actual setting, should be executed in model form with the same degree of accuracy and the same sense of construction that must characterize actual building for the stage.

Materials for model-making are divided into several classes. Structural materials used for building the framework of settings, especially in the case of plastic and irregular stages, include wood, cardboard and paper, papier-mâché, various thin sheet metals, plaster of Paris, screen cloth, wax, clay, cement, soap, sand, and other special substances. Nails and brads, papier-mâché, sealing wax, paper clips, gummed tape, string, and wire may be used to fasten the different parts of a model together. For covering structural frames, paper, cloth, cardboard, papier-mâché, plastic wood, liquid gelatine or celluloid, sand, cork, and other surfacing materials are helpful. In filling crevices in scene models, the designer will find putty, clay, wax, plastic wood, sawdust and glue, and papier-mâché to be of great service. For the final smoothing and finishing of the surface of a model, the use of sandpaper and emery cloth, and tools such as pen-knives, scissors, razor blades, and chisels will assist.

Materials for the suggestion of architectural detail are almost innumerable. Toothpicks, matches, and straws may be used for

◀ *The same model setting. These photographs show the different effects on the same setting produced by two styles of lighting.*

SCENE DESIGN—THE MODEL

window muntins, and mailing tubes, wooden dowels, curtain poles, and cardboard for architectural columns; very thin strips of cardboard will combine to suggest such details as cornices, paneling, and moulding; plastic wood, clay, wax, papier-mâché, wood, or cast metal offer possibilities for the representation of such details as capitals, corbels, caststone panels, and statuary; and corrugated cardboard forms an excellent material for the suggestion of roof tiles.

In the case of miniature box or screen settings, one of the chief things to remember is that they have to be "struck" quickly, with ease and without intrinsic injury to the units; for this reason, even in model form, they must of necessity be strong. In the event of the scenic unit being conceived as hinged flats or screens, the designer can easily employ gummed tape or cloth glued to both edges of the flats in question. This arrangement serves admirably to create the illusion of hinges.

In making models of permanent settings, the designer may firmly anchor the entire structure to a base and execute each detail with special attention to sturdiness and accuracy of effect. In semi-permanent settings, it is well to build a strong basic structure and to execute the auxiliary units, plugs, and details with finished precision. This insures perfect fitting to the setting as a whole.

In making model steps, circular units, winding stairs, ramps, platforms or other units of this nature, the designer will find

◀ *Model for* Hamlet *by Arthur Hurt,*
◀ *showing the possibilities of solving*
◀ *lighting problems by the use of minia-*
◀ *ture stage lighting equipment.*

that an application of the principles of geometry will be most beneficial in the correct planning, cutting, and assembling of their integral parts. If one is careful in the drawing and clever in the use of supporting tabs, it is sometimes possible to produce almost an entire step unit out of a single piece of cardboard. In making steps it is a good policy to cut very lightly along construction lines so that the cardboard will bend easily and accurately; this not only assures a good clean job in the end, but offers, indirectly, considerable strength to the finished model. This process can also be used to suggest hinged flats, in which case additional strength can be secured by reinforcing the entire joint with cloth glued loosely but evenly across the two members so as to afford easy movement in their use and adjustment.

In the representation of model exterior scenes, the sky is very important and should be well conceived and executed. There are several ways in which the exterior sky can be represented. A piece of cloth, colored or dyed to suggest the sky, can be mounted on brass or metal battens (curtain rods), bent to suggest in miniature the curve of the real cyclorama; the bottom of the cloth can be weighted with dress weights or finishing sinkers; and the entire arrangement may be rigged on miniature lines and suspended from the gridiron. A miniature plaster dome can be constructed by means of a wooden frame, curved at the sides and top to suggest the hemispherical shape of the sky and to afford the even lighting usually gained by the use of a

◀ *Model for* Hamlet. *Model and lighting*
◀ *by Arthur Hurt. Effect produced by*
◀ *the use of miniature stage lighting*
◀ *equipment.*

real plaster dome. This frame can be covered with screen wire and finished with real plaster, plaster of Paris, or similar substance, painted and used as a permanent feature of a model stage. A very inexpensive, less durable, but sometimes highly effective substitute for a cyclorama may be fashioned out of cardboard, bent into the shape of an arc, supported, shaped into place, and painted. It is possible to suggest the sky with a plain miniature backdrop of blue material.

Details for exterior scene models may be made with a variety of materials. Trees and shrubs can be suggested with sponges cut to shape and painted, with cork, shaped paper, or papier-mâché. Toy or actual model trees can sometimes be bought, re-shaped and re-painted. Exterior ground rows can be made of cardboard mounted on wooden strips or bent in such a way as to form a self-support; thumbtacks are often helpful in securing such units to the miniature stage floor. Leg drops and foliated borders can be made of paper or cloth, mounted upon mosquito netting or gauze, and weighted at the bottom with miniature battens or other types of weights. Tree trunks can be made of wooden or cardboard disks, covered with cloth, colored gelatine, or colored silk, and then shellacked, or they may be built fairly substantially by the use of papier-mâché. Miniature backdrops sometimes aid greatly in suggesting depth in landscape settings. Each exterior setting presents a different problem to the designer, and it is only by a complete knowledge of materials and technique in their use that successful model exteriors can be made.

The problem of representing different types of special mechanical stages in model form is not so difficult as one would ordinarily suppose. Revolving stages can easily be suggested by the use of a circular wooden stage mounted so as to rotate around a central pivot. Upon such stages model settings can be built with great permanency. Settings for this type of stage should be studied carefully, not only as individual settings, but from the point of view of ingenuity in arranging each setting so that it is economically placed upon an integral area within the whole, not allowing a unit of another setting to present a confusing appearance as a background for the setting being used at the moment, but dovetailing settings cleverly into each other for storage purposes. Elevator stages can be constructed with the use of miniature pulleys and lines or, in specially designed models, a small motor may be employed to elevate the stages. Wagon stages can be suggested by miniature trucks or wagons on toy rollers or wheels. Tracks can be made so as to insure uniformity of placement of these wagons behind the model proscenium arch. Miniature hinges, screws, screw hooks and eyes, and other miscellaneous hardware find a ready place in construction of special type stages.

The painting of models can be studied in a very limited way. Color schemes can be determined, but the actual use of them in correct relation to value and intensity can be planned only in a preliminary way. Almost all colors in the painting of actual settings undergo a considerable modification from the model painting owing to the visual effect of greater expanses, and the physical and aesthetic effect of colored light upon colored pigment. Colors represented at high intensity in miniature settings often have to be toned down, while in other cases the drab colors of a scene model have to be brightened in the real stage setting in order to prove aesthetically pleasing. This is a matter of artistic ad-

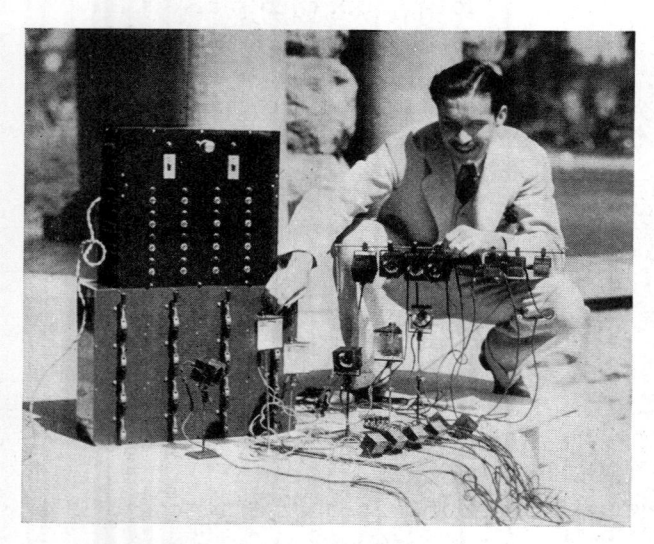

Model lighting equipment. Except for miniature olivets and control board, the instruments were designed by George Hall, Melrose, Massachusetts.

SCENE DESIGN—THE MODEL

justment and lies almost entirely within the province of the artist.

Plastic units and cycloramas which will be used over and over should be painted with a ground coat of neutral hue and then spattered with the three primaries of light—red, yellow, and blue—in order that, upon the application of any of these three colored lights, the particular hue will be evidenced in the visual effect. This makes for greater flexibility in the chromatic adjustment of model scenery, just as it does in actual settings.

On account of the special effects of colored light upon colored pigment the lighting of a scene model should be studied with particular care. In a very subtle manner, light can be employed to change the aesthetic and emotional atmosphere of a model setting. The model instruments and devices for lighting the scene model should approximate, as nearly as possible, those used in the actual theatre, especially as regards their flexible use. By the use of such equipment the designer can forecast accurately the color, the control, and the aesthetic effect of stage light on the actual setting. It is advisable to install a complete model lighting equipment built to order by a responsible manufacturer; however, this is usually too expensive except where it will be of constant use to the designer. Model switchboards and dimming control boards are available at high prices. Good substitutes for the more expensive model lighting instruments can be found in the form of the ordinary Christmas-tree lights. These of course have to be arranged in an orderly manner if used in the lighting of stage models. Sometimes the designer is able to devise his own particular lighting equipment at a very low cost; this not only offers a chance for interesting work but also affords the designer an opportunity to incorporate any special arrangement or device into his equipment. Experimentation in the design and building of miniature lighting equipment is to be encouraged among those who are interested in model stage settings.

As in sketches, some attempt should be made to suggest the scale of the model stage setting. It is a very good plan to model at least one miniature human figure for this purpose. Such materials as pipe cleaners and wire may be used for the base; this may be covered with string to afford a solid and rotund object and the whole thing covered with wax and modeled in finished form. Hair may be suggested with colored threads. Simple clothes may be easily made out of scraps of cloth. A figure not only gives scale to the model setting but suggests in advance to the audience the character of the play.

In general, every detail in the making of scene models should accurately suggest a definite treatment of materials and technique in the actual setting. In this manner a scene model becomes not just a toy for amusement but an intelligent and carefully chosen point of beginning for the scene designer, technician, and painter.

◀ *Model control board for miniature stage lighting. Plugging board designed by Harold Helvenston and constructed by John Newbegin.*

LIGHT IN THE SCENE

IN THE consideration of light, used as a medium of dramatic expression in the theatre, it is necessary that the sheer importance of such an element be first established. For this reason I think it well to recall an instance which, in itself, might have easily happened within the scope of almost anyone's experience, a case of one's recognizing, outside of the regular theatre, the power of a factor which in its modern use is so vital in theatrical production.

It so happened that one autumn day I sat in the stadium of an Eastern university watching a football game, the importance of which was manifested by a capacity crowd of over eighty thousand spectators. Decked out in colors of the respective institutions, the great human ellipse became discernible as two vibrant masses of contrasting colors; one naturally cold in hue and made more so by the frigidity of November air in New England, and the other predominantly warm in color and modified only by cool reflected light. The sun was obscured by a cloudbank.

In the field below, two struggling teams were huddled into a nondescript mass—their athletic equality evidenced by an apparent deadlock in the center of the field. It was the latter part of the fourth quarter with the score almost tied. At the moment every conceivable element was contributing to the dramatic quality of the spectacle. The air was brisk, banners and flags were waving, bands were playing, and each great cheering section was a unit in its excitement. The multitudes in the stands pulsated each development of the contest by wild shouting. The air was charged with an atmosphere alternately of fear and expectant joy. High above the stadium aëroplanes buzzed, and pilots added to the scene by maneuvering in a series of loops. Myriads of colored balloons soared upward from the stadium until the sky became a veritable kaleidoscope. Everything seemed to emphasize the great scene below: that of two human machines each straining to put over the decisive play. The very air was tense.

Then, in a gleaming flash, a player emerged from the tangled formation and darted in the direction of the goal. First one and then another opponent tried in vain to tackle him. The people in the stands became more vociferous and almost in unison stood erect—a frantic mob. The elusive player, bounding on his zigzag way, neared the ten-yard line. Visions of the inevitable loomed: the player neared the goal. There a frenzied opponent downed the runner, in a final effort to save the game. The effort was futile. The player had crossed the line. A touchdown!

And at that instant, like a miracle vouchsafed by pleasure itself, the sun blazed from behind the clouds!

The great dramatic climax had been intensified by an aura of brilliance almost too wonderful to perceive. And what happened?

A design by William Kline for a mystery play by Harold Helvenston and Eri Richardson, Jr. Notice how clearly the designer has suggested lighting.

LIGHT IN THE SCENE

The warm side of the stadium became a glorious mass of seething color, and the cold side, due to the orientation of the stadium, was left in a deep shade, frigid and formal and stiff. Ice and fire seemed to clasp hands in a moment of glory; and, then, a pistol shot proclaimed the end of the quarter and terminated a great spectacle.

The game had been won and lost during the last few minutes of play. Purely as a dramatic exhibition, the game was magnificent. Until the moment of the sun's entrance, it had been thrillingly dramatic. But, at the crux of excitement, the gods entered in to provide the finish of an already great drama—a blaze of glory almost beyond conception. It was a bit of glorious theatricality.

At that moment, I felt the joy of drama intensified to the point of greatness. The advantages of perfect co-ordination of production elements were made vivid. Circumstances had combined to furnish a model performance. Drama had progressed from the sheer dramatic to the ultra-theatric. The football game, with the sun coming out as it did, had become a revelation of the importance of well-regulated stage lighting in ideal theatrical production. It had stressed the basic elements of scene design: the value of composition with a definite focal center, the advantage of every factor and detail building to a great final climax, and, more even than that, the value of color intensified by light. In nature, I had found a scene and a stage setting into which light had incidentally entered to create a maximum effectiveness. With that experience I realized that reasonable skill in the lighting of a stage setting is not enough, that in order to achieve the most expressive results in theatrical scenic production one should demand virtuosity in the lighting of a setting.

An Idea about Light

ROBERT EDMOND JONES, in an address delivered to the students of the Department of the Drama at Yale, expressed the idea that in stage production light should be used to illuminate the actors as though that were the last time they would ever be seen; that in this manner light would serve to perpetuate the image of the actor upon the mind of the audience, thus creating a lasting impression of the drama. Mr. Jones intimated that the greatest importance of the use of light on the stage lies in the intensification of the action of a drama without ever becoming intrusive as an element itself.

Visibility, the first requisite of light

Light as the means of visibility has always been of primary importance to dramatic production. From time immemorial the actor has had to be seen by the spectator and thus has become a slave to light as far as his visual performance was concerned. Prehistoric performers necessarily depended upon the sun's rays or firelight for illumination while acting. Beginning at dawn, the Dionysiac festivals of the ancient Greeks ended at dusk, simply because of the necessity for light. Despite the fact that dramatic illumination was slowly modified and improved by the development of artificial light, natural light occupied a

◀ *Biblical scene in which a Rembrandt painting effect was desired. The actors are bathed in mellow light. Designed by Harold Helvenston.*

SCENERY—A MANUAL OF DESIGN

Scene from the San Francisco Temple Players' production of S. Ansky's The Dybbuk. *This illustrates the fine use of a single light source.*

position of great importance in stage production until the latter part of the sixteenth century, when, toward the end of the Elizabethan period, the theatre moved inside and dramatic productions were illuminated by candlelight. Artificial light had come to stay. Soon, following on the heels of candlelight, came the oil lamp and the gas light—these finally to be replaced by the electric light, the first real use of which came in the latter part of the nineteenth century.

Emotional expression in light

Generally speaking, the other great use of light in dramatic production lies in its power as a medium of symbolic expression and as an aid to the portrayal of emotion. In the Greek and Roman theatre torches were used to symbolize time of day and weather. Later on, in quest of greater effectiveness, colored light was introduced. This helped to intensify the aesthetic effect and to increase the emotional element of the drama. The development of artificial light and of instruments for its use and control has led the modern producer to recognize its possibilities as a flexible dramatic medium and an element of utmost importance in the theatre.

It is safe to say that no other one element of theatrical production has so revolutionized modern stage scenery as lighting. This may be attributed to several main factors relative to the general trend of modern drama and its production. The partial divorce of drama from realism has manifested itself in the writing of expressionistic plays of many scenes—plays which demand not only simplicity but also ingenious combination and use of scenic forms. This type of play may be mounted in various ways, ranging from a series of individual stylized settings to a single structure, different parts of which are used to represent different scenes. Modern plays have thus created a reactionary desire on the part of the lighting expert to use light as a medium of scenic expression in itself. Plays of today are written with an eye toward different permeating moods in various scenes and acts, and it is not to be doubted that light is one of the most facile agents for expressing such moods.

Color in light assists primarily in the creation of emotional and psychological effects; however, it has only been in recent years that color media have been perfected to the degree of efficient combination with light.

Special effects

Not only has science assisted in perfecting lighting instruments of wide variety in design and use, but other stage lighting equipment has been developed so as to permit a greater scope for dramatic expression in light. Cycloramas and plaster domes have been devised and painted so as to render chromatic changes in scenery easy by the simple manipulation of lights. Stage lighting companies have developed mechanical devices for the effective production of such special effects as moving clouds, waves, rain, waterfalls, fire, and other elemental phenomena.

Light projections

Scenic demands of plays by Shakespeare, Ibsen, O'Neill, Shaw, and other dramatists have caused further development of lighting

LIGHT IN THE SCENE

by means of projections. The simplest form of projection is the ordinary shadow projection, based on the Linnebach principle in which a cardboard cutout or stencil is placed between the light source and the projection surface. The result is a design in light and shadow on the projection surface. Color introduced in the stencil produces further dramatic effect.

The demand for motion in light projections generally requires an instrument equipped with a lens. The ordinary stereopticon, employing a slide, illustrates the principle of this type of light projection. To obtain the effect of motion the slide is moved by hand or by a clockwork apparatus, such as is found in the ordinary effect machine.

In the somewhat flexible use of projections the designer is able to add a great deal of

◀ *Setting for* The White Peacock, *a harlequinade by Priscilla Flowers, produced at Yale. Designed by Harold Helvenston.*

flare to scenes requiring such effects as avalanches, hurricanes, tornadoes, spectral apparitions, and architectural effects such as arches and columns.

Effects of this nature are generally projected in the following ways: from the cyclorama trough upward upon the cyclorama; from instruments set on the stage and concealed behind ground rows or scenic units; from the sides or from behind the tormentors upon the backdrop or cyclorama; from the bridge; or, in some cases, from a combination of positions.

Ordinary projections are obtained by using a Linnebach projector or similar type of instrument, cutting a piece of black cardboard to the size of the color frame slide and adding

◀ *Setting from the San Francisco Junior League production of* The Sleeping Beauty. *Photograph by Gabriel Moulin.*

color, if desired, either by gluing it actually to the cardboard or by using a separate frame in combination with the cardboard.

An illusion in light is demonstrated in the two settings here shown for the San Francisco Junior League production of *The Sleeping Beauty,* adapted by Mrs. Andrew Talbot and Mrs. William Kent, Jr., directed and staged by the author of this volume. In the first illustration the light is projected against the tower, rendering a solid, opaque effect. Note the transparent effect produced in the second setting below.

In shadow projections the design, of course, is the important thing and the cutting of the silhouette slide presents a number of problems. It is easy to see that if the light instrument could be placed so as to afford an even distribution of light rays upon all areas of the projecting surface (backdrop or cyclorama), the cutting would not be so difficult—the design projected in light would closely resemble the image suggested by the cutout

◀ *Another setting for* The Sleeping Beauty. *The tower, made of theatrical gauze, is rendered transparent by vertical strip lights concealed within it.*

SCENERY—A MANUAL OF DESIGN

Sketch for Act One, Wagner's The Flying Dutchman. *Daland's ship by a rocky shore. In this scene the background is kept dark, emphasizing the lighting of the ship. Designed by Donald Oenslager.*

portion of the cardboard. Generally, however, owing to the many physical limitations of the setting, the instrument cannot be thus arranged and is of necessity placed in a special position: down low in the floor or in the cyclorama trough, up high on the light bridge or on a teaser batten or light bridge, or, in some cases, from the sides behind the tormentors. This explains the fact that in any of these cases the image projected would be distorted in a ratio directly commensurate to the irregularity of the distance between the instrument itself and the extremities of the different areas to be lighted. Then, too, it is easy to understand how difficult it would be for the actor to avoid casting a shadow of himself upon the wall should the instrument be placed too far downstage or too low on the floor. It would mean that the actor could never use the area between the instrument and the projecting surface—a condition limiting the director's use of the acting area of the stage. The third difficulty in such placement lies in the fact that the instrument itself might be in plain view of the audience, a thing in itself distracting and uncalled for.

Therefore, in summing up the precautions to be observed in the use of such projection, I should make the following recommendations: Conceal the instrument itself; place the instrument as far upstage as possible to avoid interference from the actor in accidentally walking into the light and thus projecting a shadow image of himself on the wall; finally, try to equalize the distribution as nearly as possible on all areas of the back wall.

Since the cutting of a stencil or projection is very difficult, it is generally the best policy first to place the instrument in the actual position where it is to stay, and then to insert the cardboard in the frame and cut the stencil by the trial and error method, that is, watching the actual image change and grow into visual being as the projection is actually being made. Often one will find that the slightest cutting or trimming of the actual cardboard will bring about a great alteration in the image on the back wall and it will be found necessary to have gummed tape and strips of cardboard ready to replace and adjust any error that is made as one goes along. In this process of cutting and piecing together of the cardboard one should keep the stencil as strong as possible to avoid any accidental tearing or disrupting of the stencil while in transit or in use. It is generally useless for the designer to try to cut a stencil from a purely theoretical point of view—leisurely, as it were, at a drawing table. Much time can be saved by cutting it while the instrument and cardboard are in the actual position for use during the performance. In-

Sketch for Act One, Wagner's The Flying Dutchman. *In this scene Daland's ship is kept in silhouette against a sky made phantom-like by means of projections. Designed by Donald Oenslager.*

LIGHT IN THE SCENE

teresting color effects can be built up on the cardboard stencil by gluing bits of colored gelatine over the opening.

Another way of getting around the difficulties of distortion arising from oblique projection or from the uneven or irregular surface of the setting upon which the projection falls is through the use of the model. A model of the portion upon which the projection is to fall is constructed to scale, and the exact effect required is painted in black and white. A photograph is taken of the model section, and from the negative a slide is made which, when projected upon the corresponding portion of the full-scale setting, gives a faithful reproduction of the pattern painted on the model. This method requires considerable care in the painting of the model, since any imperfection is greatly magnified in the process of projection. Furthermore, the size of the model (to exact scale, of course) and size of the full-scale projected pattern will be in the ratio which the distance of the camera from the model bears to the distance of the projecting instrument from the setting. The projector must be directed with reference to the setting exactly as the camera is directed relative to the model.

Projections in light, as scenery, have been used rather extensively by certain European designers such as Linnebach, Hasait, and Seivert, and we find examples of their effectiveness in America in the work of Lee Simonson, Jonel Jorgulesco, and Donald Oenslager. Projections not only play a part in some stage settings, but in some cases constitute in their own right almost the entire scene. The emotional and sensuous quality of such lighting generally contributes in a distinct and pleasing manner to the scene. Projections of this kind have been effectively used in productions of Shaw's *Back to Methuselah,* Elmer Rice's *The Adding Machine,* and plays of Shakespeare, Ibsen, and other dramatists.

Mechanical Lighting Devices

PROBABLY the most startling development of special lighting machines is that of color "organs" arranged mechanically and electrically so that the operator is able to control and create imaginative compositions in light with a reasonable amount of flexibility as far as color, shape, intensity, and moving pattern are concerned. Although this type of machine offers difficulties in its handling and in its placement and use in actual production, it has been successfully employed in scenic production. The clavilux, a color organ developed by Thomas Wilfred, has been used with great effectiveness in productions of Ibsen's *The Vikings at Helgoland,* in dance drama, and in other illusory types. This novel mechanism, made flexible by the manipulation of a keyboard, will in all probability affect the future of stage lighting. It is highly possible that in time to come certain stage scenery will consist of very little more than moving light completely synchronized with the mood of the drama itself and perfectly co-ordinated with the movement of the actor. The perfection of such a machine and the mastery of it by the lighting artist will

◀ *Scene from* Creation, *a mechanistic ballet. Designed by Harold Helvenston. A spotlight below the dancer produced a huge, moving shadow.*

SCENERY—A MANUAL OF DESIGN

allow complete flexibility in the building of a complex dramatic background by the suggestion of minor moods within the play. Thus an emotional climax will be made possible by the rhythmic correlation of light with the development of the play in its entire continuity. Light will have then approached the point of virtuosity as a scenic element.

Modern lighting experts

Stage lighting, as such, owes a special tribute to Richard Wagner, one of the first who conceived of the theatre as a true unification of all of its arts. Lighting played a definite part in his music festivals at Bayreuth. Gordon Craig, the English theatre artist, decades after Wagner, recognized its use as an intensifying agent in the scene. His Swiss contemporary, Adolph Appia, was also among the first to consider light as a complete and powerful element in itself—his sketches are the embodiment of light in the scene. While a great deal of credit is due each of these three artists in their theories and practices as regards light, it took the great showman, Max Reinhardt, to realize the practical possibilities of the use of light. Reinhardt fits light into the scene as an experiment of the moment, never attempting to settle for good upon any particular style or type of lighting. He will use bold lighting in one production, in another a very subtle type, while in a third he may even show his audience the actual instruments used to illuminate the scene. Throughout all of his work he gives the impression of keeping an open mind as to the art of lighting and always chooses the form of lighting best suited to the production at hand. His experiments are revelations to students interested in lighting.

A number of important developments in stage lighting have been brought about by American designers and lighting experts. Louis Hartman, the power behind David Belasco's stage lighting, has contributed much to the perfection of instruments, reflectors, and special means of securing light effects. Munro Pevear of Boston and Charles Holzmueller of San Francisco have done a great deal toward the design and manufacturing of instruments. Vincent Duffy on the Pacific Coast is known for his ability to light outdoor pageants. Stanley McCandless of the Yale University Theatre has devoted much of his time to the thorough grounding of students of stage lighting and has contributed valuable service by way of experiments in different phases of lighting. E. B. Kirk, an Easterner, has developed a very intricate control board designed to allow simultaneous juxtaposition of color and intensity and the pre-setting of lighting continuities for entire scenes by means of mechanically arranged interlocking devices. Irving Pichel has experimented a great deal with switchboards and lighting plants in California theatres. In many places throughout the country active work is being carried on in the interest of stage lighting and its problems as well as in the designing of lighting equipment to suit special needs. One lighting expert has designed and manufactured miniature lighting equipment perfected to such degree as to be a source of great value to designers and technicians.

Types of Lighting

LIGHT is definitely employed to illuminate four main elements of the scene: actors, interiors, exteriors and skies, and, finally, special effects. The lighting of actors may be divided into four main classes: overhead lighting, footlighting, level lighting, and cross-lighting.

Overhead lighting

This method is used to produce illumination of a general type. Formerly old-fashioned light borders or metal troughs were arranged with low-wattage bulbs of different colors, regularly divided, but this method has become almost obsolete and is now replaced

— 44 —

LIGHT IN THE SCENE

by borders of concentrated flood lights, each equipped with metal grooves to accommodate color frames. This type of lighting, if used alone, is highly artificial because it illuminates only the horizontal planes of the face and body, this in turn producing very deep shadows under all such protruding features. Overhead lighting is most satisfactory when used in combination with level and cross-lighting.

◀ *An example of overhead lighting. Note the deep shadows. Christmas Play, 1930, Bohemian Club, San Francisco.*

Footlighting

Footlighting gives an effect exactly the opposite of overhead lighting in that all the nether surfaces and under portions are brought out in full light, resulting directly in a series of grotesque shadows which appear on the upper and receding parts of the face and figure. Chiefly on account of this undesirable effect, footlighting has either been combined with other types of lighting or eliminated entirely except in musical productions which require a great abundance of bright and colorful light. Modifications and exaggerations of this type of lighting are sometimes helpful in the revival of old comedies, particularly those of the Restoration period.

Level lighting

This term may be applied to lighting that comes from instruments arranged approximately on a level with the faces of the actors. The danger of this type of lighting, however, lies in the overemphasis or lack of balance caused by the intense light on one side of the actors' faces and the resulting deep shadows on the other side. In order to render this type of lighting satisfactory a balance should be sought as regards the intensity of light on both sides of the face. Monotony is relieved and interest is often gained by the use of different colors on opposite sides of the stage.

Cross-lighting

Cross-lighting may be designated as that type of duplex lighting which is generally allowed to descend directly upon the actor from opposite sides and from high downstage positions. Any color scheme conducive to the emotional element of the play and harmonious to the make-up may be used.

Interior lighting

In past years it has been the custom in the lighting of interior settings to cast light purposely upon the walls of the set. This practice was common in the period when it was popular to display the setting above everything else in the scene; however, in the present day, when better taste prevails in the matter of stage settings and the actor and the play are foremost in the mind and purpose of the producer, it is only with a subtle diffused light that the walls of an interior are directly illuminated. Of course in the matter of doorways, entrances, and special areas important to the action it remains for the lighting artist to throw a little extra illumination on the particular region. If, however, a play of a past era is being revived, it is generally well to simulate the lighting of the period in which the play was originally given. In such a case, if the lighting was traditionally brilliant, a part of the charm in the revival will lie in

SCENERY—A MANUAL OF DESIGN

◀ *A setting from* Pueblo, *written by Covington Littleton and produced by George Pierce Baker at the Yale University Theatre. Designed by Donald Oenslager.*

the artist's ability to recreate the period atmosphere of the play.

Exterior skies

The lighting of exterior skies depends largely upon the facilities of the theatre used. The lighting of a small cyclorama or sky dome can be accomplished by under-lighting from a sunken trough built for that purpose or by cyclorama units placed on the actual stage floor and arranged around the curve of the cyclorama or dome. In this type of lighting the rays project upward upon the curved surface and, owing to the proximity of the instruments to the bottom part of the cyclorama, it is natural to expect the base to be more brilliant than the upper parts of the sky. If the gridiron is high enough and facilities are adequate, it is advisable to offset such misplaced brilliance by overhead lighting. Some theatres are equipped with special cyclorama batteries; in other theatres one is forced to devise a method of lighting by the use of flood lights hung on battens or borders especially constructed for this purpose. A combination of over- and under-lighting generally affords a more evenly balanced light and makes a more convincing general effect.

In the use of floor units it is important to mask the instruments from view of the audience by means of ground rows, shrubbery, or other scenic devices. There is nothing more amateurish than to expose lighting instruments carelessly and reveal lighting methods to the eyes of the audience.

In the use of a backdrop instead of a curved cyclorama colored borders may be used. Care, however, should be taken to create a realistic color in the sky. This is generally difficult on account of the painting of the drop—a drop may be too brilliant or too dull or too low in key, so that the color and intensity of the lights must be modified to offset error and to assist in producing a convincing effect. There is little worse to look at than a very dull sky when the scene calls for bright daylight, or a lurid, artificially colored sky when it is evident that a murky or stormy sky is called for.

Lighting of offstage effects

Effects viewed through doorways, windows, portholes, and other miscellaneous openings in the setting may be lighted by means of strip or backing lights. Such instruments consist of a shallow metal trough containing a small number of low-wattage bulbs. These bulbs are generally dipped in color, thus eliminating the use of color frames. A strip or backing light should be carefully concealed above a door or window or on the sides of the opening, care being taken in the latter case not to cause dark and incongruous

◀ *Another setting from* Pueblo. *These two settings illustrate use of structural units. Lighting designed by Stanley McCandless.*

LIGHT IN THE SCENE

shadows to fall on the back wall as actors pass in and out of the opening. For this reason it is generally advisable to place strip lights above the head of the actor if possible.

In creating the illusion of bright light coming through a window or an opening, as in representing sunlight or moonlight, olivets or bunch lights should be used. The olivet is a large squarish metal hood containing a 1000-watt bulb; the bunch light is nothing more than an upright stand arranged with several low-wattage bulbs emanating in different directions from the top. In the use of such instruments it is necessary that the source of light be completely concealed from the eye of the audience; otherwise such brilliance would be very distracting to the play.

Light pockets and color consistency

Small spotlights are employed for highlighting the actors and for creating a special visual emphasis on important or intimate scenes. In using spotlights as the main source of illumination care should be taken to rid the stage of light pockets or areas where there is practically no light at all. Light pockets have the disagreeable feature of causing the actor to be seen clearly for a moment while passing through a well-lighted area, only to be almost totally lost in the darkness of another ill-lighted part of the stage. Another thing to look out for in spotlighting is to see that the colors are of the same general hue or that the difference in the colors used in adjoining

◀ *Sketch for Clemence Dane's* Granite, *designed by Frederick Stover. The lighting is obvious, coming distinctly from the fireplace.*

areas is not too great. Sometimes a production is branded as being "rank amateur" only by the fact that the actors jump from one color in one area to an entirely different color in the adjoining area.

Special effects

Sunset effects may be created by the use of olivets or flood lights fitted with louvres or parabolic reflectors. Such instruments are designed to allow the light to issue forth from them in straight, parallel rays.

Special moving effects such as fire, clouds, rain, snow, waterfalls, and so forth, may be produced by means of instruments fitted with special mechanical devices for the production of motion. Such instruments are expensive, and it is generally advisable to rent them from a stage-lighting supply house.

Flashes of lightning may be obtained by cutting out a design in an opaque color slide and using it in the manner of a projection. A very brilliant high-wattage bulb should be used for lightning effects. The illusion of sheet lightning may be secured by the flashing on and off of powerful flood lights. The thing to remember in producing such an effect is to distribute the lighting convincingly and to use the proper color medium.

Avalanches and brainstorm effects can be gained by mechanically operated disks, which, in revolving, interfere with the light projection, thereby rendering the stage intermittently light and dark. Trick sky effects requiring a great variety of color may be effected by the use of batteries or circuits

◀ *The graveyard setting for* The Adding Machine, *by Elmer Rice, designed by Harold Helvenston. Note the specially designed proscenium opening.*

SCENERY—A MANUAL OF DESIGN

of different-colored lights manipulated in a manner suggestive of the atmospheric condition desired. The changes in the color of the sky should be gradual and not abrupt. For modern plays of mood and special mental ideas such effects are not only useful but highly conducive to the dramatic effectiveness of the scene.

Lighting: Obvious and Subtle

OBVIOUS stage lighting is illumination in which the light instruments or sources are exposed to the view of the audience. Reinhardt's system of overhead lighting, in which the suspended instrument is lowered into complete view of the audience, is one type of obvious lighting. If an actor uses a flashlight for stage illumination, that is also a form of obvious lighting. Spotlights and arc spots attached to a balcony and in full view of the audience are other examples of this type of lighting. All visible floor, table, or bracket lamps are classified under this head. In some productions of recent years the entire light bridge has been lowered into complete view of the audience: that is probably the extreme type of obvious lighting.

The decision as to whether or not the lighting should be of obvious character is governed by the discretion of the director or designer or both. If the play is well made and of a realistic nature, it is easy to see that such lighting would probably interfere somewhat with the visual continuity or the aesthetics of the scene; however, in other plays, especially those in which an author is stressing an idea rather than the plot or the realism of the characters, this form of lighting has proved very helpful in the establishment of the main idea. Chekhov's *The Marriage Proposal*, in the constructivist manner as done by Hallie Flanagan at the Vassar Experimental Theatre, employed the idea of using the light bridge fully exposed to the audience—an idea which aided materially the purpose of the producer.

Subtle lighting as a term may be applied to that type of stage illumination in which the light sources are concealed from the view of the audience. The chief argument in favor of this type of lighting is that the technical details do not interfere with the play and no attention is drawn to the source unless the beauty of the scene has surpassed the other

◀ *A scene from* The Singing Minute, *by Maude Humphrey, showing much detail characteristic of the realistic type of setting. Note the mellow lighting. Produced at the Yale University Theatre by Alexander Dean. Setting by Harold Helvenston.*

LIGHT IN THE SCENE

elements of production. The average audience accepts the subtle type of lighting more readily than the obvious type, chiefly on account of its being accustomed to it in the production of realistic drama.

Obvious lighting is more likely to be appropriate in experimental and stylistic productions than in realistic or naturalistic plays. However, it is within the province of the producers to decide which method is likely to be the most successful.

Color in light

Colored light thrown on its corresponding color in pigment has a tendency to create the effect of white, that is, provided there are no different surrounding colors in view. The effect is much the same as that of seeing a white rabbit in snow or a green suit against a background of trees or shrubbery in springtime.

Pigmentary colors combined with a complementary light become dull and dark. The chromatic effect of the original color is intensified only when surrounded by lights of a color other than that of the object illuminated. Settings painted in definite harmonious sequences may be lighted with the same general type of color. Actors clad in colors complementary to the general light and intensified by spotlights will create a distinct visual contrast and a generally pleasing effect.

Attention should be given to the composition and intensity of the light transmitted through various color media. Light will penetrate such colors as straw, light amber, DuBarry pink, and very light blue quite easily. Green and red gelatine are a great deal denser, and dark blues and violets transmit an exceedingly small percentage of light.

A pigmentary secondary will reflect not only the primaries from which it is made but also the intermediate hues. Thus, magenta will reflect red, blue, and various tones of violet.

The great function of color in stage lighting is that of creating emotional and general effects.

In the lighting of general acting areas it is well to create mellow light of different colors, the form of the play and the mood of the scene always acting as the agent to determine the selection of colors. Tragedy generally calls for cool colors at low intensities—blues, greens, blue-violets, and sometimes reds. This, however, is not by any means infallible, for in a subtle domestic or realistic tragedy we sometimes find that straight lighting is most effective and truest to the play. Comedy, farce, and musical shows almost always demand warmth, brilliance, a variety of color, and general all-over lighting. High-lighting is accomplished by the use of high-powered, long-throw spotlights and arc spots, and it is generally well to use warm colors at high intensities.

Illumination: General and Specific

STAGE lighting is chiefly a matter of illuminating the acting areas and the actors themselves. In successful stage illumination the intrinsic stage setting is seldom lighted for itself alone except in instances where such illumination is needed for pictorial emphasis, as in the case of certain farces or comedies where an obviously brilliant background is needed, or in the case of a decidedly weak play the production of which is made excusable by the stress laid on its scenic beauty or charm. In almost every case the lighting should be such that it will at no time spoil the visual focality of the actor or in any way divert the spectator's attention away from the dramatic content of the scene.

It must be agreed that the essential medium of presented drama is the actor, and it is only right that full emphasis be given him by the lighting as well as by the costume, setting, and other elements of production. By this token, the actor should never be lighted so as to allow an accidental emphasis on the setting itself as the result of the actor "stepping out

— 49 —

of the light" or suddenly changing his position into an area which has little or no light.

In a broad sense stage illumination is divided into two classes—general and specific.

◀ *A scene from the Stanford University production of Karel Čapek's* The Makropolous Secret, *using simple properties and a black cyclorama.*

All areas ordinarily traversed by the entire acting group can be broadly lighted from above by using low-wattage flood lights. Standing or hanging olivets may be employed for this type of lighting. Overhead border lights and footlights have been used for this purpose, especially in musical shows; however, in order to gain a finer emphasis on the acting and to eliminate the too-brilliant-all-over aspect of this antique type of lighting we find spotlighting coming more and more into use as the finest type of selective lighting.

Specific lighting is generally accomplished by the use of high-wattage spotlights capable of throwing a concentrated beam of light at long range. This type of lighting is generally used for lighting special areas such as tables, chairs, mantels, et cetera, and also to augment the general lighting of important positions such as doors and windows.

In musical shows, concentrated illumination of a mobile nature is necessary—singers and dancers must be followed while performing. Owing to the fact that such productions usually occupy the extreme downstage area and, in some cases, the forestage, and consistent with the limitations of the placing of such lights, arc spots are generally used. These instruments are operated from a balcony or other projecting platform by skilled operators. There has been developed recently an instrument known as the incandescent spotlight, which is rapidly succeeding the arc spot for lighting musical shows. These incandescent spotlights will eliminate certain annoying qualities of the arc spot—particularly the ringing, buzzing noise.

SCENE PAINTING

PAINT, as an element in the coloration of stage scenery, is a variable factor; it may or may not occupy a position of importance. It may be subordinated in the neutral color of plastic settings, it may become flagrant in its detailed execution of the older type of painted, pictorial setting, or it may be delightfully suggestive in a fine stylized setting. The importance of paint in a stage setting usually depends upon the type of play, the style of production, the technique of the artist, and the use of light. However, as a means of assisting to create visual color, paint should always add a dynamic quality to stage scenery. Color on the stage should possess a vibrant quality; it should change in tone to correspond with the progression of the dramatic moods of the play, and for this reason scene painting should be studied carefully, not as a haphazard smearing of pigment upon a canvassed flat, but more as the highly developed art of painting unobtrusively for an ensemble effect of costumed actors moving against color in light. Thus, painting becomes a rather important part of scenic representation if carefully executed, or an imposed distraction from the play if carelessly done. For this reason, the representation of monochromatic color or flat-tone effects seemingly simple as visualized from the audience often requires very complicated processes in its execution.

In the aesthetic sense, scene painting may be defined as the art of using paint on stage scenery to create color in combination with stage light; and, in the technical sense, it is the process of using paint to approximate the effect suggested in the designer's sketch.

A sketch by Harold Helvenston for the Stanford University production of Evreinov's The Chief Thing. A good example of the use of paint and amusing design to establish the atmosphere for fantasy.

SCENERY—A MANUAL OF DESIGN

The artist's drawing is the dream picture—the graphic idea of the artist's emotional feeling about the setting. For the painter the sketch is merely the point of beginning—a keynote to the ensemble effect of everything within the setting. In order to create such an effect in an actual setting each detail has to be painted in definite chromatic relation to the rest of the setting. Charts act as guides in the selection and mixing of color. It is usually to the advantage of the designer to prepare full-size samples of color and technique desired, especially in the case of scene painting in experimental theatres where students and assistants aid in the actual execution. In professional scenic studios, however, an artist is generally safe in allowing skilled painters to work out the technique in order to secure the special visual effect of the sketch. As a general rule, technical and color charts provide an accepted reference for the painter and, when specified by the artist, should be used.

Materials and Equipment for Scene Painting

MATERIALS for scene painting are generally understood to mean pigments, vehicles, and other special substances. Since color is naturally the first desideratum, its consideration is of primary importance. It may be had in the form of oil paint, water-color paint, dye, and other miscellaneous forms. However, of these, water-color is most commonly used in scenic representation.

In painting scenery, water color is of the greatest value because it can be used not only for canvas flats and walls of a setting but also in the painting of furniture. In such cases varnish and shellac can be used over dry water-color to render a toned antique or finished effect that is waterproof and permanent and will not soil the costumes of the actor.

Water-color scene paint can be had in either dry or pulp form. Each of these has its own distinct advantages and disadvantages.

Dry color comes in bulk form so that it can be purchased in any quantity desired. A great color range is available in this form of pigment, and it can generally be had in any locality. Another distinct advantage of dry color over pulp color is that the painter is able to mix subtle tones in almost any quantity, whereas one is usually timid about using pulp color in this way on account of its expense. Generally speaking, in the mixing of colors inexpensive dry pigments are just as effective as high-priced pulp paint. Water added to dry paint makes it darker in value; for this reason, the painter should determine his color in the preliminary dry form. It will appear the same after it has dried upon the canvas.

In using pulp paint the painter is compelled to guess the value of the paint as it dries on the actual flat. Pulp paint affords the painter a more extensive range of colors than dry paint. However, because of the pure quality of the pigment used and because it is sold in small quantities and distributed in crocks, it is much more costly than dry paint. The fact that this form of paint has already been mixed with water accounts for its usual smooth quality and the pleasure that comes from working with it.

Other important materials used in water-color painting are: whiting, for giving body to color and making colors lighter; and glue to act as a binding agent and to cause flats to stretch tight and even.

Oil color is frequently used in the realistic representation of woodwork, such as cornices, paneling, dadoes, baseboards, doors and windows, and their frames. It is used a great deal in the painting of furniture and properties.

Oil paint can be bought either in tins of paste consistency or ready mixed, the latter variety being the more expensive for the amount of paint to be gained. Paint ground in oil can be made as thick or as thin as the painter desires and in this way offers a certain flexibility in its use.

Stains and japan colors are used in the painting of woodwork and furniture.

Varnishes and shellac are used for their protective qualities and also for their glossy

SCENE PAINTING

quality in the finishing of furniture. Flatting varnish is used over oil or water paint when a slight gloss is desired.

A vehicle is the liquid used to dissolve and flow paint. Of these fluids, oil is perhaps the most permanent, despite the fact that it takes longer to dry; turpentine is used in connection with oil paint principally as a means to quick drying. Turpentine has a tendency to make color dull when dried.

Special materials for covering or painting include metallic bronzes (requiring bronzing liquid or glue as a vehicle), flitter (brilliant metallic flecks used to represent metallic surfaces and used with glue as a binder), ground cork, sand, and other such substances used in the creation of special surfaces or novel effects.

Scene-painting equipment is generally understood to include containers and utensils for mixing, preparing, and storing scene paint and brushes, and other materials and devices for technical use in the application of paint.

A paint frame is a major item of equipment; however, if this is not to be had, floor space, wooden horses, and ladders are necessary for other methods of scene painting.

Containers should include wash tubs or very large cans for great quantities of paint, ordinary buckets for smaller quantities, and pans of all sizes from large tin baking pans to muffin tins and tin cups for small quantities of paint used in the painting of details.

Brushes should include the wide kalsomine variety for sizing flats and painting large masses, long-handled brushes with shorter bristles, ranging in width from one inch to two and one-half inches, for detail work, and smaller brushes for striping and for painting architectural detail.

A painter's equipment should also include lettering brushes for the painting of sharp lines, and lettering and short stiff stencil brushes for the production of fabrics and draperies for stage use. Also, under the head-

◀ *Sketch for 1927 Fine Arts Ball at Yale.*
◀ *Painted artificiality used to gain an*
◀ *atmosphere of merriment and fes-*
◀ *tivity. Designed by Harold Helvenston.*

ing of equipment come rags, towels, sponges, and other materials used in the special painting techniques. Mahl sticks, straight edges, chalk lines, and other devices are needed for scene-painting by various technical methods.

Methods of Scene Painting

THERE are three principal methods of painting scenery, each possessing definite advantages and disadvantages. The most modern method is that of the paint frame. This is a wooden frame, usually about thirty to forty feet wide by twenty-five or thirty feet high, the height of which is adjusted by means of counterweighted lines. This method has many advantages. Often an entire setting can be assembled at one time on the frame in its proper physical order so that the painter is enabled to execute the painting in one operation and with the chromatic sequence and relationship in which it will later be seen on the stage. With a paint frame the painter is able to work in a natural, erect position without excessive fatigue. The height of the frame is adjustable and the painter is not obliged to try to paint something out of his natural reach. Lights such as will be used in the final lighting of the setting can be rigged over the frame and thus the artist can see the actual effect that lights will have on the finished setting. Another advantage lies in the fact that one can stand off and view the setting from a distance and thus get a definite

— 53 —

SCENERY—A MANUAL OF DESIGN

idea of it in its entirety and as it will actually appear on the stage. This method requires the least amount of room in the workshop. The disadvantages are slight, the main one being that thin paint applied with a full brush has a tendency to trickle down and thus form a sometimes undesirable streaky effect on the flat. Another disadvantage is the possibility of drawing the release weight too high or too abruptly, thus allowing frame and all to descend at high velocity into the basement or lower floor. As a method, however, the paint frame is most satisfactory. It is thoroughly efficient and economical.

A method practiced in Europe and sometimes in America is the floor method. This type of painting is accomplished by arranging flats on the floor with space between them for walking. Painting is accomplished from an erect position and by the use of long brushes. A great deal of floor space is required, and, although it is impossible to get a complete idea of the setting, as in the case of frame painting, the painter is able to visualize the general effect of the painting. However, when the painting is done at night, the lights are generally directed down upon these flats and the brilliance of direct lighting never quite resembles the lighting used on the flats as assembled vertically on the stage. This method of painting sometimes results in the painful realization that the scenery has been painted in light more brilliant than that which will be used in production and is consequently too lurid or intense. It is also sometimes difficult to keep from walking on the flats while they are in this position. There is further a certain amount of difficulty in reaching some of the wider flats from the aisles, and with the stooping position necessary for this type of painting the painter often becomes very weary.

Another disadvantage is the danger of allowing color to pool and dry in an ugly manner, thus spoiling the general effect of the finished flat. For this reason the painter should be careful not to use a brush that is too full. A variation of this floor method is that gained by the arrangement of flats upon horses and painting from a closer and more comfortable position. The proximity of the painted flats to the painter sometimes deceives, the setting being painted for close inspection instead of for the perspective actually experienced when the scenery is viewed from an auditorium.

The third method of painting scenery is the ladder method. In this manner an assembled setting may be painted under the lighting that will be used in the actual performance. Though this is somewhat of an advantage because of the ability to get a definite unified

◀ *A scene from Priscilla Flowers'* The White Peacock, *produced at the Yale University Theatre. In this setting the back sides of flats were painted to represent a kitchen. The other side of the flats served for another scene. Designed by Harold Helvenston.*

SCENE PAINTING

effect of light upon pigment, it is dangerous and tedious and should not be practiced except in theatres which are limited in space and in special cases where a maximum solidity and chromatic unity of setting is desired. Despite its advantages this method offers perils to the painter, who is forced to work in mid-air.

Technique of Scene Painting

THE TECHNIQUE of scene painting is a matter for the individual designer to decide. The actual methods of securing a desired effect depend upon the whims and practices of the painter; different painters get the same general effects by the use of different methods. However, there are three main processes in general use: sizing, laying-in, and finishing. It is in the last stage that the painting techniques vary, and with such in mind I shall try to present all of the well-known methods.

Sizing

Sizing is the first step in painting scenery. It stretches the fabric tightly over the frame and produces an opaque surface upon which colored paint is applied.

Sizing is made by putting into a large bucket about three-quarters of a bucket of dry whiting, allowing water to flow easily into the bucket while a stirring rod or stick is used vigorously to dissolve the lumps and make an evenly consistent paste. Three or four small cups of glue are then added to this mixture for binding purposes and enough water is added to insure the proper consistency for the easy use of the brush. The amount of glue is variable and is usually determined by each individual painter in the preparation of sizing. Large flat kalsomine brushes should be used with a semi-diagonal up-and-down stroke, care being taken to use enough paint to cover the flat without slopping it on too thickly. If there is too little glue the paint will crack, and if there is too much the sizing will stretch the canvas or cloth too tightly. The whiting serves to fill the pores of the fabric and the glue acts as a binder to stretch it tightly upon the frame.

"Laying-in"

The next step is the painting of the base or ground color. The process is called "laying-in" and the paint the "lay-in." This sort of painting varies with the setting and the mood of the play. In a formal play or setting the lay-in may be of one flat color; for a comedy it may consist of different colors toned together with the brush; and for stark tragedy the painter may paint with two or three colors definitely apart and adjacent to each other, depending upon a finishing process to create a closer chromatic unity or "pull the colors together." It must be remembered that, although the selection and mixing of the lay-in colors is extremely important as the base of the setting, it is also easier to correct or tone the color later with a finishing process. In painting the ground tones the painter should be careful to assist the light with paint by making his color more brilliant or of a higher value around an opening through which light will pass, and care should be taken to paint corners of the room in a darker value than the lower and more brilliantly lighted areas.

For the lay-in a painter should decide not only what colors but also what degree of subtlety to use in the painting process.

Whether they will obviously meet and stop on the flats or whether there will be a careful blending of them in the ground coat is a matter for the artist's personal judgment. Color can be merged or blended by the sheer brushing of two colors together or by the use of water to tone them.

Finishing techniques of scene painting

Rolling.—Rolling is a finishing process gained by the use of a towel or rag dipped into paint, squeezed, twisted lengthwise, and rolled in any regular manner over the ground color of flats. It is more often used as an intermediate than as a final process in painting, usually following the lay-in and preceding the spattering process. Some very pleasing effects can be gained by this process.

Sponging.—Sponging is a painting method achieved by the use of a sponge dipped in

◀ *Setting for Pirandello's* Right You Are. *The contrast of the dark furniture with the gray setting forms a keynote to the spirit of the play.*

color and applied with slight pressure to painted flats in any regular and continuous manner. The result of this sort of technique varies with the size of the sponge used, the amount of color used, the manner in which it is handled and the skill of the painter in the use of such an instrument.

Scumbling.—Scumbling is one of the oldest scene-painting techniques. It is primarily one which employs the use of a dry brush or a brush only partially full of paint. Paint is applied by means of the end of the brush and with a light stroke; however, the manner in which a painter works is a matter of his own personal taste and skill. Scumbling softens the ground color and tones the different values of colors together. It will be found advantageous in the representation of walls in poor and middle-class houses and in suggesting wall paper in scenery. A great many different effects can be secured by experimenting with this technique. In the setting shown above, the scumbling process is used.

Spattering.—Spattering is one of the most subtle of scene-painting techniques. It is used in many different ways for different purposes and effects. Sometimes it is employed to tone in ground areas of different colors; it may be used on semi-permanent and permanent settings, plaster domes, reversible flats, screens, and any type of scenery where changes in color are affected by the juxtaposition of light (each hue in the spattering reacting definitely to different-colored light rays); it may be used to finish off scenery that has already undergone scumbling or other processes of painting. Spattering consists of filling a wide brush with paint, holding it in one hand and striking it against the other wrist or hand, causing small dots of color to fly off upon the flats. Care should be taken to hold the brush with the flat side almost parallel to the object being spattered. This insures an even effect providing the paint is evenly distributed. Too much paint in the brush will result in an uneven and messy effect. Sufficient paint should be used so that the dots will not become too small. The subtlety of spattering usually increases in direct proportion to the number and variety of different colors used, to their harmonious relation to each other, and to the skill of the painter with the method. This process is used in the setting for *Moving On* shown below.

◀ *Setting for a circus operetta. The illusion of round circus tents was gained by the intrinsic shape of hinged flats.*

Dripping.—Dripping is a special variation of spattering, and is usually done by arranging the flats upon the floor, taking a full brush of color, and allowing the paint to drip evenly upon the ground color of the scenery. Care should be exercised in the case of the use of complementary colors, for careless practice causes the color to pool in dirty masses upon the flats and often necessitates the repainting of the flats.

Toning.—Toning, as a scene-painting process, serves to link two or more colors or two or more values or intensities of the same color together without a chromatic break noticeable

SCENE PAINTING

to the audience. The process of toning scenery or color areas may be accomplished by actually brushing different colors together while in a wet state or by the use of water, a third color, or a glaze as a unifying medium. Toning gives scenery a vibrant and lurid quality and is used especially in painting scenery for fantasies, musical comedies, revues, and other types of light dramatic or comic productions. The toning process was used in making this setting for *The Queen's Husband*.

Glazing.—Glazing is a method used principally to bring about closer tone harmony and chromatic unity in stage scenery. It is usually employed as a final painting process because of its subtle technique and its value as a toning medium. Glaze is a very thin liquid made of a small quantity of color, a little glue, and a great deal of water. It is usually applied in single, direct strokes of a wide brush used in one manner and in one direction, special care being taken not to disturb or dissolve the dried color underneath. This process can be used over surfaces painted by any process and especially in the painting of reversible screens. It is sometimes advisable to add metallic bronzes to glaze. This assists color in its own illumination and often creates a very pleasing effect.

Striping.—Striping is the process of drawing straight or regularly curved and uniform lines in the representation of architectural detail and other special effects in scenery. Straight lines should be snapped with a chalk line, and a long-handled, narrow brush should be used with a straight edge or mahl stick in the actual painting.

Outlining.—Outlining is used mostly in the painting of decorative and fantastic settings where details and objects are not painted for their realistic qualities but with the idea of amusing the audience. Long-handled, narrow brushes should be used with a freehand stroke for this sort of painting.

Mask-Spattering.—This process is em-

◀ *Rococo setting for Sherwood's* The Queen's Husband *as produced at Stanford University by Gordon Davis. Designed by Harold Helvenston.*

ployed when only a portion or parts of a flat or scenic unit are to be spattered or treated. A piece of cardboard or thin wooden board is held over the area to be protected, thus allowing only the exposed portion to be spattered. Some very subtle effects can be secured in this manner, particularly those portions involving combination with light.

Painting Convertible Scenery

IN PAINTING flats or units that are to be used in different scenes, under different colored lights, it is the common custom to paint a ground tone of neutral or almost neutral gray, either warm or cold in hue, and upon this to spatter three or four or any number of different colors according to a definitely preconceived color scheme. The spattering colors may be primary colors of light or pigment, secondary colors of either, or any other chromatic system pleasing or desirable to the artist. The value of these colors should be the same if there is not to be a predominance of any one color. This, however, is arbitrary.

This technique results in a very flexible surface for lighting, and when properly combined with different hues and intensities of light it is capable of creating many imaginative and pleasing effects. If any one light hue is used alone on the scenery it has a tendency to bring out that particular hue in the setting. If two colored lights are combined, the result will reflect its corresponding combination in pigment. Thus a red light upon scenery that has been spattered with red will produce a red glow to the audience; a combination of red and blue light will bring out the red and blue qualities of the setting or their chromatic result, which is magenta. Plaster domes, used in modern theatres to represent the sky, are painted in this manner. As a method of painting, this offers the most economical, flexible, and useful type of scenery known and is especially recommended to little theatres as a satisfactory method of painting. The process can be varied in any way to suit the conditions of the theatre, the play, or the individual taste of the artist and by a process of experiment is capable of revealing many interesting scenic possibilities.

Scene-painting methods depend upon the individual artist. There are no hard and fast rules about materials, tools, and technical manners of painting. The result is the thing that counts, and to that end the painter should work, regardless of orthodox methods or preconceived ideas or prejudices concerning scene painting.

I once knew a portrait painter who mixed melted wax in his oil pigment in order to get a special texture in his paintings. His canvasses were often so large that he would lay them on the floor for painting; in order to cover some of the larger areas he would sometimes use a scrubbing brush to apply this odd mixture. His medium and his tools and methods of painting were indeed strange, but his compositions were a revelation. In one of his religious paintings the light around the head of Christ became a glowing halo of the most uncanny golden light I have ever seen. It lived. I am sure that the wax added a wonderful quality to the pigment.

This same method of reasoning applies to the art of scene painting. It does not matter how an artist or painter achieves a special effect so long as he does, and provided it is convincing and not too obtrusively artificial. The tools, materials, and technique of different artists vary in every field of art, and it is within the province of every craftsman to experiment with all sorts of materials and techniques to the end that he may discover and master the ones that best serve him in his particular realm of endeavor. This applies very strikingly to the scenic artists, of whom at one time or another almost every conceivable demand is made and whose utmost ingenuity and originality are constantly tested and challenged.

Painting Stage Furniture and Properties

GENERALLY speaking, stage furniture should be painted in strict harmony with the color and feeling of the setting in which it is being used. It is pleasing to the eye for furniture to blend quietly into a setting in the case of unimportant pieces just as it is extremely effective for a painter to create a notable contrast between the setting and any important piece of furniture. In some plays a visual emphasis upon certain pieces of furniture is required by the author and the director. Furniture should seldom be glossy or give the appearance of being newly painted unless it intensifies an idea, strengthens a dramatic value, or assists in the building of a character in the play. Some artists paint furniture with oil. Others employ water color, overlaid with a coat of flatting varnish or shellac; this treatment protects the costumes of the actors and also gives the piece just enough gloss to keep it from being dull.

◀ Neutral background for a few well-
◀ selected objects. Designed by Harold
◀ Helvenston for Michael Rafetto's 1930
◀ Bohemian Club Christmas Play.

Properties should be painted in strict

SCENE PAINTING

accordance with their use and their importance in the setting. The same general rules and ideas of furniture painting apply in this case. Sometimes color helps to gain an emphasis for the object itself and is necessary, but for the most part properties should become an integral aesthetic part of the setting and should not intrude themselves.

Painting Architectural Detail

IN THE painting of architectural objects the painter should determine the importance of detail and execute it accordingly. In many cases it is better to suggest architecture than to try to paint it in full detail. Meticulous architectural detail is seldom pleasing to the audience and then only in the case of its having been done by an expert skilled in this type of work. In any case it is within the power of the artist to decide the manner of representing architecture in scene painting. In the case of three-dimensional real detail, such as actual cornices, mouldings, and pediments, the general rules of color harmony and value contrasts should be observed and followed.

Painting special effects

Wood and graining.—In representing woodwork in scenery, care should be taken to create effects of quiet suggestion rather than of painstaking detail. Graining, if done at all, should be done with restraint. Drybrush strokes can be used to excellent advantage in suggesting the grain of walnut, oak, and similar woods. Graining tools are sometimes used, but on account of their mechanical nature and artificial results should generally be avoided. In representing mahogany a very good effect can be gained by painting a ground coat of the most brilliant hue of the wood itself, then going over this with a darker tone of red, and finally with a slightly wet brush washing and penetrating through to the inner brilliance, allowing the under coat to come through. Sometimes a very slight grain can be suggested with a dry brush of a darker red.

Marble.—In the painting of marble for the stage, show-card colors are usually the most useful type of pigment, chiefly because of their smooth opacity and the ease and pleasure which comes from their use. The ground colors of marble should be more brilliant than those actually found in nature on account of the carrying qualities demanded of scenery and on account of the use of artificial light. Ground color can be laid on and water

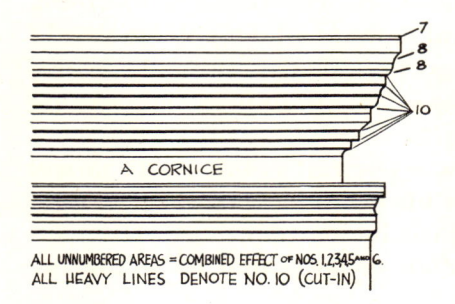

SKETCH SHOWING METHOD OF PAINTING ARCHITECTURAL DETAIL IN SCENERY.

LEGEND

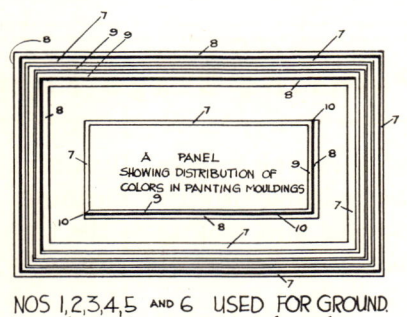

NOS. 1 AND 2 LAY-INS (EDGES WELL BLENDED TOGETHER)
NOS. 3, 4, AND 5 ARE ROLLED ON WITH RAG
NO. 3 LOOSELY.
NO. 6 SPRINKLED OR SPATTERED WITH BRUSH.
NO. 7 IS LIGHT.
NO. 8 IS SHADOW WHICH IS GENERALLY COOL.
NO. 9 IS REFLECT OR SHADE AND IS GENERALLY WARM.
NO. 10 IS USED FOR CUTTING SHARP SEPARATION LINES.

or thin paint used to tone or glaze the colors together. The veining of marble should be done with a fine red sable brush. The designer should decide whether or not he wants to create the effect of marble which has all come from one stratum, or whether the marble shall match in the reverse manner from a common center line in the case of a fireplace or mantle. If he chooses the latter idea, then he should be careful to repeat the design of the veining in duplicate on the two sides of an area abutting at a common center line. In general the color of marble as well as its veining should be exaggerated somewhat if the designer desires it to be recognized.

Stained glass.—Stained glass can be represented in silk and painted with dye; it can also be made of other fabrics, treated first with linseed oil, allowed to dry, and then painted in oil colors to conform to a design; or it may be synthetically built up out of colored gelatin such as is used in stage lighting. The leaded partitions should always be definite, complete, opaque, and usually black or dark gray.

Ordinary glass can be represented by using white translucent rayon silk or other light fabrics to be either toned with light-colored dye water or treated with liquids to gain transparency. Screen cloth or fine mesh wire, either bright galvanized or blue copper, may also be used to represent glass. The metallic substance affords just enough surface to create a slight reflection, and the possibility of light reflection into the audience is eliminated.

Stone.—Because of the infinite variety of stone, the many possible natural colors, the various geological formations, and the manner in which stone is cut and used, it remains for the artist to work out his own technique for this type of scenic representation. If three-dimensional stones are made of papier-mâché or some other substance, it is the part of the artist to supply only the color and the slight augmentation of natural light and shade effects. However, if stones are to be painted on a flat drop or wall, the artist is challenged to create not only the color but also the perspective foreshortened and the complete light and shade illusion. Stone should be painted with little attention to meticulous detail and with as much imagination and quiet charm as possible. Note in the illustration below that the stones in the wall are not tediously drawn but simply suggested.

Other effects.—For special effects a scenic artist should experiment and exploit different materials and technical methods of representation. It is from this phase of theatre work that some of the greatest pleasure is derived, and deceptive possibilities for scenic representation are certainly unlimited.

A scene from Milne's The Ivory Door, *as produced by Harold Helvenston at Stanford University. Setting by Frederick Stover.*

THE EXTERIOR SCENE
The Natural Exterior

THE PSYCHOLOGY of the audience should be taken into consideration in the matter of designing scenery, especially exteriors. The average audience accepts interiors more readily than exteriors, either because there is a certain sameness to the average interior or because of the limited knowledge of most audiences as regards period design. The average American would naturally accept as correct an eighteenth-century drawing-room done in the French manner—usually because he has never seen one. In taking anyone out of his particular environment into a strange surrounding, the artist is usually safe with even an adequate representation. But with exterior settings it is different. Nature is more or less familiar to all, for everyone has had some chance to observe common botanical forms. Each has his own idea of a tree or a mountain, and it is very hard to represent these common objects satisfactorily unless the artist has been fairly true and sincere in his use of artificial materials. In some cases it is very risky to represent trees simply by their trunks or a forest by a single tree, even though the play calls for, or suggests, such treatment. Localized settings, moreover, must be accurate in detail and feeling, especially if the production is made in the particular vicinity of the setting.

Another important point to be considered is the use of real objects as part of an exterior scene. It is generally recognized that under artificial stage lighting most real objects become deadened in visual effect. A real log cabin on a stage has a tendency to look lifeless simply because the natural color of the logs is not affected by stage light as it is by the even, natural light in which it is ordinarily viewed. Bushes and flowers always become dull under artificial light; hence it is better to avoid the real objects altogether and, in their place, to employ good artificial varieties of materials which, when properly painted, will combine with stage light to produce an effect that is realistic if not more striking than the actual object viewed under its natural light. The only exception is, of course, in the production of outdoor pageants and presentations, in which one usually finds it necessary to support the scene or augment the properties with real landscape effects.

The creation of convincing exterior illusion being so difficult, I consider it desirable to set down a number of suggestions about

A proposed scene for O'Neill's The Emperor Jones, *designed by Frederick Stover. Tall tree trunks and vines are generally a problem to the designer.*

SCENERY—A MANUAL OF DESIGN

the materials to be used, the details of presentation, and so forth. Before any detailed treatment of these ideas, however, there should be emphasized the necessity for knowing and adhering to the general laws of botanical structure. The designer should remember the relationship of each integral member of a botanical form to its whole. He should study roots in their relation to the size, texture, and radial formation of lesser roots; he should know tree-trunk shapes and the relation of the trunk to the roots, subsidiary branches, et cetera; he must understand the formation of limbs and branches, their textures, shapes, and relation to foliage; and, finally, he should have some knowledge of shrubs, leaves, blossoms, fruits, and berries in regard to their formation, color, and relation to the seasons. Now for the detailed information.

Botanical Effects Used in Stagecraft

NEEDLESS to say, the exterior requirements for a play like O'Neill's *Beyond the Horizon* are very different from those for *The Emperor Jones* by the same author. The outdoor setting for *An American Tragedy* is entirely different in nature from that required for the picnic scene in *Porgy*. Musical comedies require a kind of exterior effects different from those used in a farcical musical revue, just as the exterior setting for a play like *The Merry Wives of Windsor* should be conceived in a key different from those used in a Gilbert and Sullivan operetta such as *The Pirates of Penzance*. The average exterior setting calls for the simpler botanical forms such as trees, bushes, grass, and sometimes flowers, and for that reason particular stress will be laid on these. However, owing to the latitude of modern authors and to their intricate demands I shall include the special varieties.

Grass.—The effect of grass can be secured in a variety of ways. If the designer wants to represent grass economically he may cut a piece of canvas or cloth to the size needed, painting it in greens and browns to represent the earth, and, by means of glue, apply strips of green crepe paper, shredded to imitate short rows of blades—the length of the row, the length, width, and type of blade to be determined by the necessities of the scene. This may be glued in a straight and formal fashion or in a haphazard manner leaving patches of earth showing through, the type of grass to be in keeping with the character of the exterior. After this type of stage grass has been trodden upon by the actors, the illusion it creates is strengthened somewhat by the suggestion of shadows such as are commonly found in real grass. The even artificial quality is modified. For a short-run show this type of grass serves adequately and entails very little expense in the making, the usual cost being about fifty cents a square yard.

Artificial flower companies manufacture a raffia grass; however, it is obviously artificial and a trifle regular in character. The color offered in this form of grass gives a disturbing chromatic note in the setting; it is usually too green. In general, it is the most lasting variety and also the most expensive, costing about three dollars and seventy-five cents a square yard.

Another illusion of grass is secured by the use of green velvet mounted on forms. For certain realistic settings and for operatic scenes this material finds a ready place as a quiet, pleasing substitute for grass; moreover, as a bit of color in the setting, it is usually more satisfactory than the other varieties. Painted grass on canvas is a very poor method of representation, despite the fact that it is regularly used in stage scenery, especially on backdrops.

Vines.—Usually one is able to procure almost any variety of vine from an artificial flower store; but for a designer who is compelled to make a vine, the following suggestions are recommended. After studying the type of vine for botanical structure, foliage, and flowers, a twine should be selected of the size of the main vine stem. This may be of a

THE SCENE—NATURAL EXTERIOR

good natural color or may be dyed to suit and, if necessary, stiffened by the aid of glue. Leaves can be designed in several different sizes for the sake of natural variety and transferred to green fabric (preferably cambric or muslin) that has been dyed green and stiffened on its back side with glue. Each of these is then cut out and attached to a short piece of twine (stiffened or limp, depending upon the effect desired) and this attached to the main stem. Sometimes wire may be used to attach the leaves to the main vine and thereby act as a lesser stem. Individual vines may then be tied together and arranged so as to give clustering effects or other special formations. For remote decoration leaves need not be detailed; however, should the designer wish to vein the leaves he may do so by placing the leaf on padded material and describing the veins with a hot, blunt instrument. Leaves may be backed with stiff materials if necessary. Sometimes, for minute vine and leaf detail, wire covered over with colored thread is used for the stem. Almost any species of vine may be made in this manner, and the cost is almost negligible.

Plants and flowers.—Plants must be considered from several points of view because of their infinite natural variety and the manner in which their shapes may be modified. Plants may be of the natural rambling type at one extreme or of the clipped or grotesque type at the other; the type depends upon the character of the scene and the ideas of the designer in the use of them in a setting.

Wild plants may be made somewhat in the manner of vines, the chief differences being that a plant, instead of conforming to a plane or surface and depending upon a foreign unit for support, is usually made of sufficient strength to support itself. In general, wild plants radiate from a central stem. Stiff wires may be used as radial stems. The main trunk may be formed from a shaped piece of wood (in cases where the trunk itself is visible to the audience) from which emanate the smaller stems of wire or, in some cases, smaller wooden branches or limbs. Leaves can be made by a method similar to that used for making vine leaves and assembled by means of wire or in other manner to the trunk. In making plants, it should be remembered that the individual leaf assumes greater importance as an element of decoration and that it is often necessary to represent leaves in complete detail. In the case of the elephant-ear plant and other tropical species, strength of the individual stem and semi-rigidity of the individual leaf become matters of importance, and the difficulties arising from their representation can be overcome to a large extent by the use of strong materials, stiff wire, and good glue.

Formal bushes may be fashioned on wire frames shaped to size and design. A wooden support is placed in the center of the frame, extending down into a pot, tub, or other unit. Commercial ruscus, which may be secured from any artificial-flower company, is used to cover the wire frame. The average cost of this type of bush, two feet in diameter, is three and a half dollars. Ruscus can also be used for formal hedges or clipped foliage formation. It is expensive, however, when used in quantity.

Bushes of an informal character may be made out of cloth or paper leafage or foliage formations, wired and fastened to any basic framework of wire. Such foliation may be used to advantage even on flat units, especially in cases where three-dimensional foliage is needed for a garden wall which has been represented on a backdrop. Painted tissue or crepe paper may be used as a simple groundwork for shaped leafage, the detailed leaves being fastened to the ground material. Shredded crepe paper forms a satisfactory and inexpensive material for hedges, especially in cases where they are to be seen from a distance. Clipped yew and other formal varieties of shrub may also be represented in this way. If the exterior effect is to be placed in the downstage area or if it is designed for a scene in an intimate theatre it is usually better to execute foliage in more truthful detail. For such representation leaves can be purchased from an artificial flower company in single form or in clusters. This type of leaf is permanent and accurate in detail and offers variety in size and type; however, this material is expensive and should be employed in a thrifty manner.

Flowers furnish an interesting problem for the stage designer. Artificial flowers are gen-

SCENERY—A MANUAL OF DESIGN

erally to be had in almost any variety; roses, sweet peas, wistaria, daisies, and blossoms of all kinds are the most common artificial flowers. This type of flower is more durable in its use on the stage and also very expensive. In

A garden setting for Robert Powell's Brief Candle, produced at Yale. Designed by Frank Poole Bevan. An exterior requiring a large tree.

case economy must be observed, flowers can be made by the stage craftsman, the materials necessarily varying with the floral type.

Crepe paper can be used effectively for flowers needed as static decorations, in vases and in flower boxes; however, this variety is not so effective when the flowers are handled or worn by the actor. The edges of paper petals may be rolled or curled by means of a spoon or a hairpin. Paste may be used to stiffen or wrinkle the petals of paper flowers. The petals may be formed into complete blossoms and these in turn fashioned on wires with leaves. Hollyhocks, dahlias, chrysanthemums, and other large and fairly stiff flowers are effectively made of crepe paper. For more delicate flowers, such as pansies, orchids, violets, and roses, velvet and velveteen should be used because of their natural luster, their strength and durability. Stiffened silk can be combined with velvet to produce such flowers as the iris and the orchid. Chrysanthemums of the large, long-petaled variety can be made of sheer voile, georgette, or similar material. Practically any flower of a drooping nature can be fashioned in this manner. Organdie is a valuable material for use in making flowers of a crisp yet delicate character and is especially practicable because of the ease with which it may be handled—in this respect it is next to paper in its use. It takes painting easily and can be manipulated by the amateur without much trouble. In general, the materials for artificial flower-making should be considered from the points of view of texture and color, degree of stiffness, possibility of adhering to paint and dye, and, last but not least, expense. In garden exteriors it is wise to augment home-made blossoms with a few good artificial flowers, especially in the case of such varieties as hollyhocks and larger varieties which will, in all probability, be scrutinized closely by the audience. Gardens, as a whole, can be fashioned in any style or plan, out of clusters and special formations. Artificial flowers can be made to fit holes in a wooden strip attached to a ground row; they may be fastened to any bit of plastic scenery; they may be glued to an individual base of some kind or merely set upon the ground in units, pots, or other containers.

Trees.—For small trees one may, for the sake of structural basis, use actual trees, conforming to the artist's design by combining artificial foliage with them and repainting the whole unit. Sometimes a small tree may be stripped of its real foliage leaving the trunk, to which artificial foliage is added. This method insures a strong, convincing structure upon which to build the shape and effect desired in a tree. Another variety of small tree may be made of wooden strips bound together into a specified shape by means of stiff wire. To give it a smooth surface this rough frame can then be entirely covered with papier-mâché. Lesser branches can be fashioned in the same manner and fastened to the main trunk. To the entire frame, leafage can be added by means of wire, and the whole tree can be painted or sprayed the desired color. Trees can be mounted upon a base or to any plastic, topographical or special scenic unit, for example, a fence or the side of a house; or they may be attached to the bare stage floor by the use of foot irons, bolted to the base of the tree and held firmly in place by means of stage screws. Italian cypresses, cedar, birch, and juniper trees, for decorative use, may be bought from artificial-flower companies at considerable expense, depending largely, however, upon size and amount of detail.

THE SCENE—NATURAL EXTERIOR

In large trees the trunk alone offers a difficult problem, which, however, may be met in a number of ways. Ordinarily the framework can be constructed of wood and executed in half-round fashion—or at the most, three-quarter round. Half round or round pieces of wood are sawed out for the diameter of the tree. To these along the edges are fastened vertical supports. Around the entire wooden structure canvas is tacked. Then such materials as papier-mâché, cork, shavings, sawdust, and other miscellaneous substances may be glued to the trunk to give the effect of the texture desired. Paint is then applied to this. Roots and branches may also be made in this same manner. If a large tree must be represented, it is better to build the roots and branches separately and contrive them so as to hook on to the main trunk; this arrangement saves storage room and offers protection to the more fragile details during the process of scene-shifting. In instances where the tree must be of sufficient strength and solidity to support actors, a solid wooden substructure should be made as high as needed for practical use. Of course, there is the old conventional "cut-out" tree. This may be either of flat construction, with shaped edges made of plyboard or similar substances, or it may take the form of canvas cut out to suggest foliage and glued to theatrical netting. Conventional foliated borders of canvas may be used above any trunk formation to produce the effect of density in foliation.

It is wise sometimes in the representation of wind-blown trees, in deserts or the northlands, to get a dead tree and sever its branches, rearranging its members to fit the design called for by the artist. A broken branch can be shaped with little trouble and bolted or screwed through the larger member. In rough joints papier-mâché may be used to afford a smoother surface. This method sometimes saves a great deal of time in the building of an entire tree and offers at the same time the basic quality or surface of the actual tree used.

Weeping willows require a different type of foliage from most other trees. Drooping or hanging foliage forms the most picturesque detail of this variety and care should be taken to preserve the charm found in the original. Artificial-flower stores should be able to furnish or make up the foliage detail. This type of tree is most useful in Oriental exterior settings. In other types of Oriental trees, the gnarled trunks and special textures can be secured by special basic construction and by the use of special materials for texture.

Artificial palms of almost any variety may be purchased from artificial-flower companies at a price ranging from five to thirty or forty dollars, according to size. Palms may be constructed by means of preparing a main trunk, to which commercial palm fronds are attached. The trunks of palms are usually characterized by natural horizontal circular growths signifying the age of the tree itself. This is especially true in the case of the cocoanut palm. Royal palms are marked by a rough lower surface and very smooth upper trunk. In constructing palms or banana trees, the fronds may be made of such materials as raincoat fabrics, glazed chintz, rubber, paper cambric, and other glossy and semi-stiff fabrics. The frond is first shaped in its entirety, then shredded and attached to the main structural rib. It may then be painted in the case of plain natural-colored cloth, or, if it is already green, it may be treated with shellac or other liquid to gain the desired finish. Individual fronds can be made to fit into holes in the main trunk if necessary, thus affording not only an opportunity for facile handling and striking but a system for conserving backstage space. In tropical scenes the designer may use real palmetto bushes, mounted in the fashion directed by the scene and painted to combine with stage light in producing the de-

◀ *Design for the tropical island setting of Cushing's* The Devil in the Cheese. *Note that there is no figure in this drawing to give it scale.*

sired effect. If necessary this variety of plant or palm can be made along the same lines of construction as other plants, care being taken to use convincing materials.

In a more stylized representation of tree, especially in cases where only the tree trunk is desired, canvas cylinders weighted either by round disks or by round iron rings may be used. This is not very satisfactory except when used on a "space stage" where only a bit of detail is used and scenic objects are merely suggested. Elm trees and other straight-trunked trees can be devised in this fashion.

For fantastic trees, such as are conventionally used in some forms of musical presentations and in dramatic fantasies, the flat wood-wing or cut-out can be used effectively. Symbolic trees may be represented in any number of ways and with a variety of materials. Frames covered with gauze, paper, or gelatine may be combined with light to suggest trees. Colored shadow projections in light may be most effectively employed to represent trees, especially from the point of view of emotional suggestion.

In general, trees should be studied from the point of view of their character in regard to truthful representation of detail, their function in the scene, emotional effect, practicability, and cost to the producer or designer. Each exterior presents a different problem in detail and should be approached from the point of view of its special character and solution as scenery for the stage.

Jungles and forests.—Jungles can be composed of trees in the half-round, clustered bushes, hanging vines, rushes and reeds, grass, flowers, and berries—all of these fused together in pleasing pictorial composition. Air plants and moss enhance the effect of certain types of tropical jungles; the latter can in some instances be faked with silk yarn, string, or waste, whichever variety is most suitable for the proximity of the scene to the audience. Care should be taken to anchor the trees thoroughly to the stage used in a jungle scene, unless a convincing plastic formation is used. Only too often, this type of scene is a temptation to carelessness, especially for the designer who plans mostly for orchestra sight lines. He will allow his trees to remain loose from the floor, the masking shrubbery concealing the defect from the persons sitting directly before it but perhaps revealing the discrepancy to those in the balcony. A painted backdrop or sky cyclorama may be used to augment this type of jungle setting by affording the illusion of depth.

The representation of forests in stage settings is dependent upon the play and style of direction. The means for producing this sort of effect are almost inexhaustible. In more formal productions, full-round, three-quarter, or half-round trees may be used. Sometimes geometrically shaped trees may be employed to good advantage. Fantastic forests may be represented by the use of conventional cut-outs and two-dimensional, flat constructed, painted trees. Another type of forest may be suggested by a plastic ground formation without trunks, and nothing but leaves above to set the keynote. Semi-circular, draped curtains (with jagged holes pierced through for the suggestion of light pattern through the branches) form an excellent means of giving the illusion of a forest. In extreme stylized settings a forest may easily be suggested by the use of colored projection in light.

Fields and marshes.—I know of no better way to represent fields of grain than to use the actual objects—grain stalks, cat-tails, tall grass, etc.—dried, mounted upon horizontal wooden strips and painted. The strips can be set up in any desired way, care being taken to furnish clear alleyways for the passage of actors within and behind such effects. Certain commercial grass and materials sold by artificial-flower companies can be composed into units by tacking and glueing them to wooden strips; such units are excellent for the representation of rushes and short grass. Sawgrass for scenes in marshes, swamps, or everglades may be made by cutting strips of canvas about two or three feet long and an inch wide, sewing a stiff piece of florist's wire down the middle of each blade, gluing it for stiffening and cutting to finished size, and, finally, painting them realistically. These may be mounted on a ground row or upon slender boards as the particular case demands. In extreme cases of simplified representation, such effects may be produced by the aid of light, either in a misty, hazy effect or more

THE SCENE—NATURAL EXTERIOR

concretely by the use of projections or slides. There are many forms of materials for use in connection with this type of setting, and the designer's ingenuity and ability to adapt the substituting materials to his need, coupled with actual skill in the detailed making of the integral parts, will determine the degree to which he accomplishes the desired result.

Topographical and Geological Effects Used in Stagecraft

Topographical and geological scenes require such effects as fields, moors, steppes, wastelands, deserts, sand dunes, hills, mountains, water effects, rocks, gorges, ravines and canyons, with or without water at the bottom, and caves and subterranean passages. The manner in which details of such scenes are executed depends a great deal upon the type of drama, its style of presentation, and its importance in the scene. In general, the basis of any of these effects (with the exception of water) is a wooden substructure made with sufficient strength to carry the weight of the actors and planned so as to facilitate the action necessary for the play. The wooden frame should be covered with boards for any surface which functions as a floor for the actors; it should then be padded with a substance called "ozite," canvassed over, and painted the desired color. If a special surface is required, such substances as cork, sand, and papier-mâché may be employed to advantage, the selection of the materials depending upon the effect wanted. Practical hills, tops of mountains, rocks, and similar effects are easily made in this fashion. For dressing the stage near the cyclorama, low ground rows of flat construction can be used. Sometimes a backdrop can be painted to add to the effectiveness of such a scene; in this manner of combination solid structure, flat construction, and backdrops can be used together to create the complete illusion. Sometimes the cyclorama may be used to greater advantage than pictorial representation, the cyclorama serving in its plainness to emphasize the shape of the formation and the pattern of the moving actor on top of it. Cliffs can be constructed in regular flat fashion, covered with wire and canvas, and finished either with textile materials or paint or both. The same method of construction is available in the case of rocks, care being taken to render all practical surfaces solid with flooring and padding and devising a manner by which the unit may be successfully anchored to the floor when in use. Papier-mâché or canvas stretched over wooden frames may be made to represent caves. Stylized representation of this type of effect might easily be suggested by semicircular drops used with lights.

Real water in the form of rain or running streams may be used only at the expense of special equipment, trouble, and inconvenience. Water may be represented by any glossy, light blue substance not too obviously artificial. Water outside of a ship may be suggested by a ground cloth painted the color of reflected sky in the water, the ground cloth being made to join the cyclorama or sky drop at the floor, thus completing the illusion. Care should be taken to relate the color of the reflected sky to the water in a realistic fashion; that is, the water should ordinarily be painted a trifle darker in value than the sky.

Special effects, such as race tracks, sand beaches, and so forth, can be represented by a ground cloth painted and finished in the materials best suited to texture and color needed.

In summing up this subject it is necessary to say that, in any case, the means by which exterior scenic effects are represented are directly dependent upon the conditions confronting the designer and his ability to use materials with a clear knowledge of stage technique and the use of light in scenic representation. The materials possible for use in connection with this type of setting are innumerable, and a great many interesting effects can be gained as the result of experimentation with new materials and the development of skill and technical practice.

THE EXTERIOR SCENE
The Architectural Exterior

THE PLANNING of exteriors of an architectural nature requires a clear understanding or feeling for the historical period and style of architecture suggested by the locale of the play. It is not always necessary to reproduce carefully the exact proportions of an architectural unit unless of course the object in question is well known to an average audience; and for practical reasons it is generally useless to attempt the use of actual materials in such construction. However, if the settings for a play correspond with the locale of the production, an audience familiar with the territory and its architecture and details will subconsciously demand a more or less faithful representation. For example, if the setting is that for the first scene of Shaw's *Pygmalion* and the production is being made in London, it is only natural that a London audience should demand a convincing effect of the façade of St. Paul's Church. In this case a careful study should be made of the actual building, the approaches, the number of steps arising to the entrance, their proportion, period style, grouping of columns, and all such details. The actual size of the units of such a setting should be modified only by the size of the stage. If the stage is large enough to permit the use of full-size units, so much the better; but if the stage is diminutive in size, the architectural units should be made smaller in proportion. In such a case the scale suffers somewhat — the columns may appear to be dwarfed too much by visual comparison with the size of the human figure. Such a result may be fatal to the aesthetic effect of the scene. It is well to remember that the size of the actor is constant in the eyes and mind of the audience—normal people are of one general size—and it is by comparison of the figure with other units in the visual scene that we arrive at the scale of the setting itself. If the architectural units are too small to be convincing, then the designer will either have to be content with the showing of only a part of the actual-sized exterior or he may compromise on a scale smaller than the actual but still convincing when combined with the actors. In the latter case the effect of the proportion will be visually but not actually the same as the original.

From the other point of view, that of reproducing a building of a general type, the designer's problem is of a different nature. Let us take for example a flat in East Side New York, such as is required in Elmer Rice's *Street Scene*. As long as the designer creates the general effect of such a flat, the success of the setting is reasonably assured. True, in the original production, it is said that the author had a certain brownstone house in mind and took the designer to the actual house for the purpose of reproducing it for the setting.

In a play such as *Street Scene* the designer has two main problems: first, his duty to the author and director, that of providing every practical and physical unit necessary to the action of the play; second, to create an artistic setting, authentic in general architectural detail, color, and atmosphere with respect to the particular section of New York with which the author deals. A setting for *Street Scene* is a little more general in its type than that of the St. Paul's Church setting for *Pygmalion*, yet there are certain characteristic details

THE SCENE—ARCHITECTURAL EXTERIOR

which contribute definitely to a truthful representation of that particular neighborhood.

In going down the scale from specific exteriors to general ones, a designer often finds a scene described in an extremely general manner, such as "A Street in Rome" or "A Hut in the Ozarks." In planning such a setting the designer's main requirement is that of creating the general atmosphere of a Roman street or the basic effect of a hut in the Ozarks. The proportions of the buildings themselves should be followed more in a general manner than in a specific one. In such a case, however, the physical requirements of the setting should be considered before the aesthetic effect is touched upon or planned.

Authenticity of scale is one of the most important factors in the designing of architectural settings. As a general rule it is better to represent only part of an architectural setting than to create the entire effect in a ridiculously small scale. In details such as doors, windows, arches, and units in close proximity to the actor, the designer should be very careful to create an acceptable comparison of actor and unit in the mind and eye of the spectator. For example, it would be utterly silly to design six-foot main doors for a Park Avenue drawing-room setting or a room in Sans Souci Palace. The audience as a whole would feel such an incongruity. Some would feel it consciously, while others would be subconsciously annoyed by it. A very low ceiling in the same style of setting would be equally ill-designed. In the case of a stage limited in size the designer should re-design the setting to fit all physical conditions as well as to meet an aesthetic standard.

In some plays the artist is allowed complete freedom in his work because of the extremely general demand of the play or author. In scenes such as "A House," "A Tomb," "An Alleyway," especially in modern plays of an abstract nature or in plays of expressionistic character, the designer is not even held to the conventions of locale: he may interpret the scene in terms of the idea back of the play, adding, of course, his aesthetic conception.

An exterior setting designed by William Kline for Talbot Jennings' play, No More Frontier. *This drawing is really nothing more than an elevation. It is highly artistic, yet the architectural details and scheme of lighting are clearly shown.*

SCENERY—A MANUAL OF DESIGN

Setting for Retreat, *written by Grace Dorcas Ruthenberg, designed by Phyllis Lin. An example of the realistic architectural exterior.*

In all design, we find that the use of line and mass contributes an emotional or mental quality to the work; that ornamental detail offers a keynote to the historical period, era, and locale; that scale suggests social position and color gives the sensuous motif. It is the same in architecture, and that is the reason why a designer should make a complete study of his subject before designing an architectural stage setting. In designing architectural interiors the artist should pay a great deal of attention to scale, perhaps even to a greater degree than he does in the design of an exterior—this because of the greater intimacy between actor and background or surroundings. Perhaps the effect of people in their true surroundings enters into the question. The element of scale is always immediately important in the establishment of social position and wealth of the play characters. From the moment the curtain rises the audience thinks of the characters in terms of their surroundings. A very small doorway in a spacious interior or a lavishly designed window in a poor house would in all probability destroy the otherwise convincing illusion of the scene and the acting. Such poorly planned details would probably act as a psychological obstruction to the understanding of the play.

One of the most important factors in designing an architectural exterior is the decision made by the artist as to whether the setting will be solidly constructed or painted, or, in the case of a combination of practical and painted units, how much will be practical and how much painted. Several elements must be considered before the decision is made. If there are many scenes in the play it stands to reason that the building of heavy and cumbersome practical units will obstruct the speed of scene-shifting. On the other hand, if the setting is used throughout the play no thought except that of economy should be given the design. The greatest effectiveness will obviously lie in the faithful execution of practical detail, especially in the case of one-set shows in which the audience is required to look at one background for the entire play.

If the play is extremely light in vein or if it is of the operetta variety, the designer sometimes finds an excellent opportunity to use painted scenery, especially if it is executed effectively. At times the obvious "painty" quality of scenery stresses the idea of artificiality in the play and thereby assists in creating the mood of the production. There are many degrees of reality in scenery, ranging from the "honest-to-goodness" real article which is generally expensive, heavy, and impractical, to scenery which by its very obviousness is intended to impress the audience as a thoroughly artificial effect. Some of the most successful scenery is the result of combining the real with the artificial. The scene-designer's problem is to determine the exact degree in which the real and the artificial shall fuse together. The solution to the problem should come as the result of a sensible and mutual understanding between the director and the scene designer. Many plays conceived as artificial or satirical pieces have

An architectural interior for Wings over Europe, *by Robert Nichols and Maurice Browne. Directed by Harold Helvenston. Designed by Frederick Stover.*

— 70 —

THE SCENE—ARCHITECTURAL EXTERIOR

become drab by the use of realistic settings, while other realistic plays have been smothered in flagrantly artificial backgrounds.

The modern scene designer generally feels that to eliminate detail without destroying truth is one of the first steps toward attaining a sense of good taste in stage design. In such a manner the artist uses the main motifs and patterns and tries to eliminate judiciously and artistically the non-essential details. This practical treatment is especially applicable in the case of settings of an architectural nature. Thus a cornice becomes simpler in scenic form than it is in actuality, and heavily detailed units are redesigned to eliminate the non-essentials without destroying the general feeling of the period and style. One of the greatest lessons for the amateur designer is the use of economy in the selection of architectural detail. Such procedure results in production economy as well as the cultivation of good taste.

ECONOMY IN COST OF CONSTRUCTION AND MATERIALS
General Considerations

ONE OF the most difficult problems which faces the producers of amateur plays is that of financing and controlling the cost of scenery. This is particularly true in the case of the newly organized group of amateurs, none of whom have had much experience in the preparation of a budget and the difficult job of adhering to it. The following analysis is an attempt to offer an approximate guide for the estimation and control of scenic expense in the first-class amateur production. The assumption is made that plays are produced at intervals of approximately one month.

In analyzing the costs of scenery in amateur productions, it is almost impossible to apply the cost accountant's usual principles of burden distribution. This is partly a result of the nature of the business itself, and partly due to the fact that in amateur production the number of performances of each play is not regular but limited, usually to one or two. Thus, in a sense, the fixed charges, as such, are practically nil; and the operating charges are of such a varied nature, depending upon the type of play and its own peculiar requirements, that a special segregation of them must be made. It is most convenient to divide the scenic expenses of productions into two groups: expenses chargeable directly to plays, and overhead expenses, which should be distributed annually.

Direct charges

The first general item of direct charge is salaries. The second is expense of scenery constructed solely for the production at hand. The expense of salaries comes closer to being a fixed charge than any other item; such costs should be very nearly constant. In an amateur production the scene designer is usually in charge of all the details of mounting the play; the scenery, its design, construction, and painting all come under his supervision. Added to this are the properties and sometimes costuming and stage management. The lighting of the setting is also hand in hand with the scenic presentation, and generally the electrician or lighting expert is immediately under his direction. The scene designer is indispensable in an efficient organization and should be compensated well for his services.

The amount paid a scene designer depends upon several main factors. The first matter for consideration should be the question as to whether or not he is steadily employed by the organization or group. If he devotes all of his time to the art and technical direction of the plays, his salary should be higher than if he is merely acting in an advisory capacity or is called in only at odd times for his services. Second, the executives of the organization should consider the source of their stage and building crews. If, as in a great many cases, most of the actual construction and backstage work is carried on gratis, or for academic credit by students of the organization, or by individuals interested solely in gaining practical experience, it stands to reason that a scene designer should receive a decent salary for his work. A thriving organization should also be in a financial position to pay a reasonable salary to such an artist. Third, the

ECONOMIC CONSTRUCTION AND MATERIALS

salary should vary according to the degree of regularity with which plays are produced, the number of plays produced each year, the number of performances of each play, the size of the house, and the scale of admissions charged for performances. In general, the salary of the scene designer should be proportional to the financial receipts of the organization. If plays are produced at irregular intervals, it may be found more satisfactory to pay the designer a fee for each production instead of a salary. In the case of a regular yearly program a salary would, of course, be more satisfactory to both the organization and the designer. On such a basis a good scene designer should receive from $2,000 to $3,500 a year.

In some organizations the technician is expected actually to manipulate the switchboard and operate the lights for each production, and this in addition to his various other duties. Such an arrangement is sometimes disappointing and generally offers unforeseen conflicts; in consequence it is earnestly recommended that a separate man be employed as stage electrician. This not only insures the best in lighting but also allows each department head to do his own work in an unhampered manner, which makes for efficiency and effectiveness. An electrician should be employed on the basis of a nominal fee for each production. This fee should cover his work over a period of at least two dress rehearsals prior to the performance. If the play is performed over a definite period of days or weeks, a salary should be worked out on the time basis. Generally, for a single performance, including the dress rehearsals, the fee is from $15 to $25.

Generally speaking, in amateur organizations salaries are limited to those paid the scene designer and the electrician. However, if need should arise for extra salaries to be paid and these salaries pertain to the scenic end of the production, such expenditures should be included within the budget under the heading of "direct charges." For musical productions it is often found necessary to bring in extra technical assistants, such as arc-spot operators, switchboard operators, or general utility men.

The other main item of direct charges is that of "scenic expense." Scenic expense includes the cost of scenic construction and the rental of special properties and electrical equipment. These items are the most variable costs with which the business manager must contend, and are consequently difficult to esti-

◀ *Sketch for W. Hasenclever's* Wanted:
◀ A Gentleman. *This is a suggestive set-*
◀ *ting for the park scene. It is simple*
◀ *yet easily understood. Designed by*
◀ *David B. Rossi.*

mate or control. The most satisfactory budgeting of scenic expense can be attained when there is some sort of expense control arrangement between the manager and the scene designer. In many cases the designer is informed of the figure allotted to scenery on the current budget and is instructed not to exceed that figure. An arrangement of this kind is probably the most satisfactory method of all, especially to the financial heads of an organization. The strict use of a budget generally results in a very excellent training for the scene designer.

The scene designer should submit a complete and carefully figured estimate of the scenic expense of a proposed production. In cases where students or novices do the work and labor is free, such an estimate should range from $100 to $500. In the production of a simple one-set show, the cost should be closer to $50 or $100 than $500; but in certain cases when a complex play calls for a great many scenes or for special staging apparatus or machinery it is permissible to approach the

SCENERY—A MANUAL OF DESIGN

maximum estimate for scenery. A two- or three-set show generally costs from $200 to $300. There is no infallible rule concerning scenic expense and generally no definite way of telling beforehand exactly what the backgrounds are going to cost. In a production such as *Street Scene* the designer has the problem of designing and building a so-called "one-set" show but the physical requirements and the architectural detail necessary for a convincing setting for such a play are very likely to cause the cost to mount greatly above the average cost for a single setting. In other productions such as *The Adding Machine* or a Shakespearean play of many scenes the general expense rule is in many instances exploded, especially when the artist finds a clever way to combine scenic units into the many scenes in the Shakespearean play or contrives to invent several simple but effective scenes for *The Adding Machine*. The scenic requirements of each play and production are different, and general rules are constantly broken either by cleverness in being economical in designing a many-scened play or by carelessness in devising a single extravagant setting for a generally simple type of play. Sometimes a setting may cost very little in itself, but the artist finds that special proper-

◀ *Setting by Frederick Stover for Katherine Clugston's* Finished. *Details such as alcoves, bay windows, et cetera, always run up scenic production costs.*

ties or necessary furniture for the play will run his expense sheet up above his expected figure. On the other hand, the intrinsic background may cost a great deal, but the furniture or properties are practically negligible, thus cutting down expense on another element of the setting. There is no rule for determining the exact amount a setting will cost; however, there are a few basic figures which, through the careful process of minute observance on the part of the scene designer, have come to aid a business manager greatly in his estimation of the scenic expense of the production.

In comparing the cost of single interior settings the designer has found that the expense may be reckoned on the basis of the number of special units in the setting or of the amount of detail involved. It is a known fact that plain square interiors of a general size cost about the same, but the minute a stair-

◀ *Design for a backdrop for jazz music. Note modern abstract treatment of central design. Designed by Harold Helvenston for a musical revue.*

way or an alcove is added the cost jumps. Any elevation in a room such as a landing or platform necessarily increases the cost. Arched windows and openings always cost more than square or oblong ones. Windows that open or slide up and down always cost more than those that are put in solely for visual effect and decoration. Three-dimensional detail such as cornices, paneled doors, window ledges, baseboards, dadoes, and other actual details generally cost more than double the amount of a painted detail. Hardware, extra lumber, and added labor all contribute to this extra cost. In conclusion, it is perfectly sound to assume that any practical or working unit, any three-dimensional unit, or any special unit immediately increases the cost of a setting.

There are other strange observations to be had by experience in designing and building scenery. For instance, a single box-setting of the eighteenth-century French period painted, and containing very little actual three-dimensional detail, would probably cost less to con-

— 74 —

ECONOMIC CONSTRUCTION AND MATERIALS

struct than a hovel or dugout of the same size, well-executed throughout in actual detail.

In certain special cases, it is allowable for the scenic expense to run higher than the limits described above. A musical revue, for instance, involves a large amount of special scenic units, platforms, and hanging scenery such as backdrops, borders, and leg drops. The additional expense would of necessity increase the scenic budget to a figure between $400 and $500.

Charges to future plays

In many instances certain pieces of semipermanent equipment are purchased for use in a play. Such equipment may take the form of a new cyclorama or new draw curtains, a set of parallels and platforms, extra stage braces, a new dimmer or two for the electrical department, or other devices. Such equipment is very expensive in its original cost and afterward may be found useful in almost any production or at least in several productions during the year or season. Obviously, it would be unfair to charge the entire cost of such an item to the current play. For this reason the charge is set up in a separate account, and distribution is made at the end of the year either to plays which have used the equipment in question or, in some cases, to all the plays covering a certain period. The total amount of such a charge to be transferred to each play will vary from year to year, but will average from $50 to $150. In this manner a certain amount of scenery and effects can be added each year to the permanent equipment of the producing organization.

Budgeting

The importance of the budget in controlling the cost of scenery cannot be overestimated. The only intelligent method of arriving at production costs and controlling such expenditures is by the use of a budget. The following scenic budget headings are typical for use in the average amateur production: Salary of scene designer or technical director; salary of electrician or lighting expert; stage construction for current play; property construction; rental of properties or other items; electrical equipment; prorated charge of permanent equipment; personal expense of general labor staff. By "personal expense" is meant railroad or bus fares of members of the working crew, transportation charges, express charges, hauling charges, and other cash disbursements which cannot be conveniently handled by means of requisitions.

Requisitions

The purchasing or rental of all merchandise used in the building or composition of the stage settings should be handled by means of official requisitions, dated, described in full, and signed by the business manager, or, as in the case of some organizations, by the designer or technician. By this method the business manager and the scene technician are able to tell at all times the cost of scenery to date and thereby to maintain a regular control on all technical expenditures.

General recommendations

It is always well to try to utilize any old units of scenery that might be lying idle in a basement or storeroom. It is even wise to look over all existing equipment before designing the settings for a new production. Often by keen foresight a designer or technician is able to find a valuable unit which, if incorporated

◀ *Designed by Harold Helvenston for a backdrop in a musical revue. The motif is the human face.*

into the original design, will not only save a great deal of expense but also a great amount of physical labor. Storerooms should be maintained to be kept alive, to draw from

— 75 —

when needed, and not as cemeteries for old scenery. The clever designer keeps a "live" section of flats and units at all times and thus, by the use and adaptation of these flats, he is able to save a great deal of money, some of which can be used in furthering other scenic projects and details. Generally speaking, to be economical is to improve one's reputation; and often, by clever and economical planning of new units and by the adaptation of old units as part of a new setting, the designer develops the quality of creating simple and effective settings which alone distinguish him as an artist of good taste—a reputation much to be desired.

It is extremely wise to investigate the cost of materials at different places of business. Sometimes lumber can be bought more cheaply at one yard than another; and this applies to other necessary materials and equipment. It often happens that the kind of lumber or material the designer has used in the past in another section of the country is a precious commodity in the particular section in which the production is being made; in such a situation the designer or technician should try to find material just as good, or "almost as good," but cheaper on account of its being native to the section. It always pays to shop and investigate prices before buying construction materials. A dollar saved on one commodity is a dollar more profit on the show or a dollar more to spend on some other item of scenery.

Stage Building Materials

TECHNICAL materials are divided into three main divisions—structural, covering, and hardware. Under one of these heads may be found all the materials necessary in scene construction.

Structural materials

Structural materials include all materials which are used for frames or covered to make acting structures, supports, or backgrounds. Thus platforms, stage rock foundations, stairways, ramps, and flats are all structural frames, supports, or backgrounds.

The most-used material for such construction is wood. White pine is the wood most valuable to the scene-builder, but in some sections of the country it is cheaper to buy redwood, cypress, or other varieties, although the latter-named varieties are not as good. In building scenery for an extremely short run, or in building for a one-set show where the setting will remain in place throughout the entire period and not be subject to a lot of vigorous and careless handling, it is wise to substitute cheaper and second-rate materials for the expensive better grades.

Common sizes of lumber necessary to the scene-builder are: $1'' \times 3''$ for general flat construction up to 16-foot heights (for higher scenery a larger, stouter stock should be purchased, such as $1\frac{1}{4}'' \times 3''$, or $1\frac{1}{4}'' \times 3\frac{1}{2}''$, or $1\frac{1}{2}'' \times 3\frac{1}{4}''$); $1'' \times 2''$ stock may be used for inside diagonal bracings or toggle bars and very small construction. For a section of straight-run stairs the following sizes of white pine should be used: Carriages $\frac{3}{4}'' \times 10''$ actual size, treads $\frac{3}{4}'' \times 8''$ actual size, risers $\frac{3}{16}''$ profile board. Window muntins may be of any desired thickness: $1'' \times 1''$, $\frac{3}{4}'' \times 1''$, or even smaller, such as $\frac{1}{2}'' \times \frac{1}{4}''$. For parallels all uprights and cross pieces should be of $1'' \times 3''$ stock and all braces of $1'' \times 2''$ stock. For top of parallels the flooring should be of white pine, number 2 common, $1'' \times 6''$, tongued and grooved barn sheathing. For fireplaces, $1'' \times 3''$ is generally used, but $1'' \times 2''$ stock should be used whenever it offers sufficient strength. Baseboards along the base of a setting are usually made of $1'' \times 6''$ stock with a moulding tacked to the top. Cornices are generally built up of a number of mouldings, nailed together and also nailed to a block, especially cut to the rear form of the assembled mouldings. Mouldings for paneling, mantelpieces, and small cornices can always be selected from the regular stock of any lumber yard.

In stage construction the wooden members of a unit are fastened together in either of

ECONOMIC CONSTRUCTION AND MATERIALS

two ways: in the highest grade and most durable type of building the mortise and tenon joint is employed throughout; however, owing to the fact that such construction requires special machinery, amateurs generally resort to the other method known as butt-jointing. In this method the wooden frame members are placed in position and fastened securely by means of corner blocks and keystones. Corner blocks are right-triangular blocks about ten inches on the horizontal and upright sides and about thirteen inches on the hypotenuse. Keystones are shaped like a keystone about seven or eight inches long, three inches wide at one end, and tapering off to about 2½ inches at the other. Both corner blocks and keystones are made of three-ply wood and if bought commercially cost about thirteen cents and seven cents, respectively, exclusive of shipping or transportation charges. Amateur scene-builders will do better to buy sheets of three-ply paneling board about 5 feet by 2 feet, dividing it into twelve-inch squares, and then diagonally bisecting the squares into triangles and sawing them into corner blocks. At a cost of approximately 65 cents at any lumber yard a sheet of ply-board can be cut into twenty corner blocks ordinarily worth $2.60. Keystones can be made in the same way, thus saving great expense in a very necessary item of construction.

It is a good policy to save as much money as possible on the milling of lumber, especially in the case of an organization fortunate enough to own electrically driven planers and saws. Milling always costs extra money and is often found to be very expensive.

The scene technician should understand the difference between "commercial" sizes and "actual" sizes. A commercial 1" × 3" generally measures ¾" × 2¾", the quarter-inch of the thickness and the quarter-inch of the width having been lost in the milling or planing of the original 1" × 3". For first-class construction the technician should procure actual 1" × 3", in which case the lumberman must begin with a size larger than that in order to finish to the desired dimensions. In cases of temporary scenery or whenever economy is of greatest importance to the production, "commercial" 1" × 3" will generally be found to be of sufficient strength.

Covering materials

Covering materials include all cloths or materials used in covering flats, backgrounds, or acting structures. Canvas is the most commonly needed article for covering scenery frames. Real canvas of a good grade is very expensive (about eighty-five cents a yard exclusive of transportation charges). For the amateur, muslin or sheeting at a lower price of from forty cents to 55 cents a yard makes a very serviceable and durable covering for flats. Burlap is sometimes used for rough surfaces. Silk (or its substitute) and linen are sometimes used in the representation of stained glass or other translucent effects.

In the building of a practical stage rock capable of withstanding the weight of actors, the frames are covered with chicken wire and this covered with canvas. In some instances where a less noisy effect is desired, the frames of a practical rock are covered with chicken wire or flooring, covered with ½-inch or ¾-inch felt padding or ozite, and then covered with canvas. Paneling in doors can be made of canvas, beaver board, or what is known as three-ply wooden paneling. The last is light, durable, and easy to work with. Screen wire, either galvanized or copper, is used to represent glass, and is tacked to the rear of window frames. Such a material gives the effect of glass without the ordinary distracting reflection. Paper is sometimes used in the covering of flats, but such material is fragile and obviously lacks durability.

Hardware

Hardware includes ordinary items which may be purchased at any hardware store, and special hardware peculiar to the stage and especially designed for such use and purchasable at any stage supply house. Under the former heading we find 1¼-inch clout nails (square in section for purpose of securing purchase in wood) for use in building flat frames; cut tacks (generally No. 4 or larger) for use in tacking canvas to frames; two-inch back flaps or pin-hinges used for many purposes in stage building (especially useful in building detachable units or folding parallels); strap hinges (used in a special bent fashion on all doors opening offstage); rim locks (inexpensive locks for use on all doors opening offstage), shingle nails for smaller construction; and many other miscellaneous materials suitable for the special needs of the scene technician. The prices of such commodities are generally standard and usually very little money can be saved by shopping for this kind of material.

Stage hardware includes ceiling plates for use in assembling the members of a detachable ceiling; foot irons, fastened to the base of any cut-out, ground row, or unit intended to remain upright upon the stage; S-hooks, for keeping several flats all on the same plane from the rear side of the setting; lash cleats and screw eyes for use in the rigging of flats for lashing together from the rear side; stage screws for fastening into the stage floor or through eyes of stage braces or angle irons for the purpose of maintaining rigidity or supporting any scenic unit in its proper place onstage; special ball-bearing rollers, suitable for attachment to any cumbersome piece of scenery or special unit which has to be rolled into place in setting from offstage; and numerous other special devices and items of hardware used mainly in stage work. It should be remembered that in small towns it is difficult to procure such special items, and the technician often finds it necessary to order them from a neighboring supply house or from another section of the country. If such is the necessity it must be remembered that not only is an extra transportation expense involved, but there is apt to be a delay in shipping which would cause disappointment to the user and add to the inefficiency of the technical department. The prices for such articles are fairly well standardized, and in a great many instances there are substitutes for some of the special devices. Although it is nice to have special equipment, a great deal of money can be saved by using such substitutes in the building or rigging of a stage setting.

In conclusion, a scene technician should be as careful of expenditures of this kind as possible, ordering only such equipment as he needs, and utilizing all his knowledge in substituting cheaper articles or devices whenever possible. A great measure of the scene-technician's success lies in his ability to create effective settings economically.

THE STRANGE CASE OF SCENERY

WHAT is modern scenery? The answering of this question forms a problem of far greater importance than the casual theatre-goer realizes, however much he may have noticed the changing of styles of scenery and the tendencies to exaggerate or disregard the use of scenic decoration. One can come at the problem only by considering these changes in style—not only the changes of the last fifty years, great as those are, but the changes that have occurred from the very beginning of stage decoration. Those modifications, for the most part, have not been matters of whim or sudden invention, but changes which have taken place in an orderly sequence during the entire history of European civilization. To understand modern scenery it is not necessary to reconstruct the whole history of stage decoration but rather to sketch rapidly the development of stage settings as an essential element of dramatic production. Indeed, for centuries there was little change in scenery, and the development of stage decoration began after the medieval period.

In primitive times, when story-telling or native dances occupied the place of drama, it is probable that natural landscapes furnished the backgrounds for performers, and perhaps, when night came, the glow of a campfire became the only scenic effect. The action itself was paramount; something was to be related and the setting became incidental. However, since we must be content with only theories about the drama of this pre-historic period, our knowledge of scenery and its importance then remains vague.

We have more information upon the early theatrical performances of the Greeks. Strange to say, profound as the development of drama was in ancient Greece, the stage setting remained of the starkest simplicity. Ironically enough, our modern word "scenery" is developed from the Greek σκηνή, the background of the theatrical performance in the Greek theatre; completely subordinated to the actors and the poetry of the piece, it amounted to no more than a legendary device for entrances and exits of the actors, a convenient place for dressing and changing costumes, and a sounding board to enlarge and project the voice of the performer.

The Roman stage was nothing more than a flat imitation of the Greek architectural stage with additional embellishment introduced to heighten realistic effect. The church formed the stage of the medieval period and was, in itself, just a convenience for the presentation of liturgical drama. The development of the stage setting was negligible except for a system of "mansions" or box-like stages which came as a development of the church setting.

Modern scenery, as such, began in the fifteenth century in Italy, where we find the introduction of specially constructed wings and drop curtains, both painted in artificial perspective to represent architectural and rustic scenes. This was the first instance of stage settings being used as a complete dramatic entity and viewed through a single, large proscenium arch. The fact that all of the settings were of an exterior nature is curious and interesting. During this period the stage setting lost its incidental significance and came to be known as stage scenery.

Stage settings of the eighteenth century indicate little development from the wing settings of the Renaissance. It is true that they were conceived and executed on a grander scale, that decorative ceilings and arches were added, and that scenery, as a whole, became massive in size and splendid in adornment.

Interior scenes were introduced at this time. Elaborate stage machines and well-planned stage management offered great variety in scenic effects. The box-setting came as a final development of the wing-type interior. Finally, efforts toward greater realism in scenery resulted in the replacement of flat, painted effects by solid three-dimensional units.

Dramatic presentations of the eighteenth and nineteenth centuries were marked by the growing importance of stage decoration; in fact, scenery soon came to be an element of distraction from the play and from the general unity of effect. The natural consequences of this flagrant artificiality in painted settings brought about the last extreme of the realistic school of scenery. Classified under the heading of naturalism this scenic development had for its chief factor the use of real objects instead of artificial properties. This type of surface realism began to be practiced in Europe and America, the process sometimes becoming both expensive and troublesome to the artist and producer.

Out of the chaos of the paint and artificiality of former realistic settings and out of the skin-deep realism of the naturalistic school arose an insurgent school of producers and designers known as Expressionists, who sought to simplify the stage in one grand gesture toward refined taste and vivid dramatic emphasis.

From this general group emerged a tangent group known as Constructivists, who sought, by the abolition of decoration from the stage and the use of specially built acting structures, to afford a greater intensification of dramatic action. Stairways, ramps, and platforms were built with complete disregard of decoration; stage settings became nothing more than special stages, individually designed for each play. Other modernists concentrated upon curtains, screens, and units of various shapes and forms as means of scenic expression. Light, even in its abstract use, became so important as a means of creating dramatic atmosphere that a number of designers began to use it as the dominant factor in modern scenery.

Expressionist designers everywhere sought to suggest the stage setting and symbolize the dramatic mood of a play rather than to represent the full detailed scene upon the stage. However, it remains for some designers, even in this modern day, to continue with the old practices of realistic representation, and we still find examples of fully detailed settings, some of them painful in their exactness and others composed with an idea of refinement and reserve. And so, in the theatre today, we find an intermingling of both realistic and stylistic settings; and modern scenery is made difficult to grasp because it exists in a turmoil of these forms combined with new types of plays, new theatres, and revolutionary technique in theatrical production.

Some of the people important in the theatre have created definitions of scenery which are true and beautiful and, perhaps more than anything, expressive of themselves in art. Those definitions and ideas, expressed in elusive terms, suggest the mystery of the theatre itself. Varying slightly in context, these personal radiations provide a basis upon which one may form an individual opinion. As a whole, they may be likened to fledglings fluttering around their nest, testing their potentialities in an attempt to find complete power in flight.

Adolphe Appia, a Swiss insurgent of stage design, is known for two main ideas regarding stage settings. One is his desire to remove from the stage all unessentials, thereby allowing perfect focality upon the actor; and the other is his opinion of light as probably the most important element in scenic production. Appia is a practical man, known for his work in fusing the various elements of Wagnerian opera. His significance for future generations of scene designers is probably exceeded only by his modesty.

Gordon Craig, English designer, candidly states that scenery is only "one division of a phase of theatrical art"; that action and the voice are the other two elements which concern the artist of the theatre; and that these combined harmoniously with scenery produce artistic dramatic productions. Mr. Craig urges original self-expression, the prohibition of painted artificiality in the scene, and the development of a fine sense of exaggeration along natural lines. His conception of scenery is that it should be splendidly imaginative, strong, and poignantly expressive of the play

THE STRANGE CASE OF SCENERY

concerned. Douglas Ross, dramatic director, is quoted as having said about Gordon Craig: "So far as scenery is concerned the guiding principle of Mr. Craig is that scenery is not to be seen. Rather is it to be felt. It assists to an atmosphere instead of obtruding as a picture." It is well-known that Mr. Craig is not a practical scene designer. However, the fact that he has exerted a great emotional influence upon scene designers of the last two decades cannot be disputed.

Robert Edmond Jones, eminent American scene designer, likes to think of the scene as "the wind that quickens the flame of the play." Scenery, in his estimation, is successful if it definitely contributes to the play and, in its subtle, unencroaching charm, is dismissed in favor of the action of the play.

Lee Simonson, of the Theatre Guild, has explained the problem of scenic design as a search for the most dramatically expressive forms for play production, with particular regard to the physical limitations of modern stages.

Sheldon Cheney, critic, says: "Stage decoration, in simplest terms, is the craft of creating an adequate and appropriate background for theatric action."

I like to think of scenery as a background of living mood for the actor: "background," because an actor must have some sort of background whether he wants it or not; "living" because the scene subtly alters its pattern with the movements and moods of the actor; and "mood," because in every drama and in every scene within a drama, a definite mood is required and should be suggested.

Time has proved that scenic background can take almost any form. The form, however, matters not; the materials matter not; the color, line, mass, or lighting matter not, if the play and its action have been forcibly and dynamically emphasized. Moreover, the most beautifully painted setting in the world counts for nothing unless the play has been assisted and clarified. Highly imaginative scenery is worthless in certain types of drama, while in others it may fit the mood of the play perfectly. Scenery is universally important only as an intensifying agent of the drama, and seldom is it of major importance except, perhaps, in the case of a feeble play, or as a support to innocuous acting. It is a subtle instrument in the hands of the artist and director and should be used by them primarily as a vital support for the actor, who is, after all, the mediary between the author and the audience.

THE SCENE WEBSTER

Abstract setting. Any setting in which decorative motifs in their natural form are greatly modified, exaggerated, or obscured.

Act curtain. The curtain or drop lowered or drawn between acts.

Acting area. A space designed, constructed, or left practical for acting; any area of the stage floor, within the vision of the audience.

Apron. That part of the stage which extends in front of the curtain line; the forestage.

Architectural stage. Any stage with permanent basic features inspired by or derived from architecture.

Artist of the theatre. Anyone who contributes to the theatre through the medium of his own particular art; an author, an actor, a designer.

Asbestos (asbestos curtain). The foremost downstage curtain set between the act curtain and the auditorium. This is made of asbestos or metal and is lowered in case of fire.

Atmosphere. In scenery, the emotional or mental suggestion offered by a setting.

Back drop. Any cloth curtain used across the back stage either as a masking device or a decorative unit or both.

Back flap. A hinge, the pin of which can readily be removed in order that two pieces of scenery formerly joined by it may be separated.

Backing. Any flat or unit used behind an opening in the set to mask the backstage and add to the aesthetic effect of the basic setting.

Balcony. The area just above the orchestra equipped with seats for spectators.

Batten. An iron pipe suspended from the gridiron, to which scenery is attached. Battens are also made of wood.

Batten clamp. A special stage hardware device to fasten curtain or drops to a batten.

Blend. To effect a closer chromatic relation between adjacent colors, color and light, or any two or more elements of stage design.

Book-ceiling. A ceiling which collapses in the middle and is elevated in a V-shape to the ceiling by a single batten.

Border. Any cloth suspended above the stage to mask the "top works," act as a decorative unit, finish off a set at the top, or perform all of these functions in a stage setting.

Box-setting. A setting whose main characteristics are two side walls, a back wall, and a ceiling, all perfectly joined together.

Bring up. To raise the intensity of stage lights.

Building carpenter. The foreman of a stage building crew.

Ceiling cloth. The cloth covering the wooden ceiling frame.

Chalk snap line. A cord covered with chalk used to snap a straight line between two points. These lines are employed in the painting of architectural cornices, borders, and details.

Clout nail. Iron, flat-head nails, sectionally square—used in fastening corner blocks and keystones to units of flat construction.

Cold color. Color which reveals a predominantly negative emotional effect. Any chromatic variation ranging from green-yellow at one extreme through the greens and blues to blue-violet at the other extreme.

Color sketch. A scenic sketch showing actual colors to be used in the painting of a setting.

Constructivism. A naïve form of modern stagecraft based on substantial, acting structures, designed to intensify dramatic action instead of furnishing decorative scenic background for the actors.

SCENERY—A MANUAL OF DESIGN

Convertible unit. A piece of scenery which can be used in different ways to create different scenic effects.

Corner block. A right triangle, made of three-ply wood, used to fasten wooden members of flats together.

Cover off. To mask; to hide from view of the audience.

Cradle. That part of the counterweight system which is used to contain the weights balancing the attached scenery.

Cross section. A drawing of the view through the thickness or depth section of building construction.

Cut-in. The line used in painting architectural detail to show the division between three-dimensional moulding and the flat surface of the main plane in panels or cornices. The painted line used to denote the separation of the main plane from the special raised or lowered frame units.

Cut-out. A ground row.

Cyclorama. The curved cloth extending around the two sides and back of the stage. The cyclorama is generally painted or dyed blue and is lighted to represent the sky in exterior settings.

Cyclorama trough. A permanent trough built in below the level of the stage around the cyclorama, or dome, and used to conceal the lights for the cyclorama.

Decor. Stage settings, including furniture.

Designer. In the theatre, the artist who designs the settings, the costumes, and sometimes the make-up and lighting.

Detail. An elevation or working drawing of an integral scenic unit or part of construction, usually drawn larger than one-half inch to the foot.

Dim. To lower the intensity of stage lights.

Director. The individual who combines the arts of the theatre into a finished production, placing just emphasis on its different elements and unfolding its plot. He perfects a dramatic machine for the revelation of his own conception of the play.

Dock. The storage space for "live" scenery.

Door flat. A flat containing an opening for use with a door unit; a flat containing a door; a flat containing an opening used as a doorway.

Downstage. The section of the stage nearest the curtain or apron; a term applied to an actor's approach toward the footlights.

Draftsman. The craftsman who prepares working drawings from the elevations and sketches of the artist.

Draw curtain. A curtain in two sections, rigged in such a way that they draw horizontally on or off stage in unison and overlap in the closing to exclude the audience's view of the stage.

Earth colors. Colors that are the product of earth substances; for example, yellow ocher, raw and burnt sienna, raw and burnt umber, the qualities of which are suggestive of earth.

Expressionism. A modern movement in theatrical production which calls for the most vivid expression of dramatic ideas; the dramatization of abstract emotions. In expressionism the stage is stripped of its unessentials, and significant symbols are employed to express the meaning of the play rather than the intrinsic scenic background.

Finish off. To complete the painting of a setting by the application of final details.

Fireproofing. A fire-resisting liquid used on flats and scenery in compliance with the rules and regulations of fire underwriters.

Flat. The commonest unit of scenery, usually made in the form of a wooden frame covered with fabric.

Floor cloth. The cloth used to cover the stage floor; the ground cloth. This generally tones in with the setting.

Fly. To hoist a flat or scenic unit by means of rope or wire lines from the grid.

Fly gallery. A platform from which the various rope lines and battens of the gridiron are manipulated.

Flyline. A continuous rope beginning at the pin rail, threading through pulleys at the gridiron, and fastened to a batten or a unit of scenery.

Flyman. A stage hand operating flylines.

Foot iron. Steel stage device used to fasten scenic units to the floor. The free end is fitted with a hole for the use of a stage screw; used to prevent scenery from sliding or slipping along the floor.

Forestage. The apron of the stage; that part which extends in front of the curtain.

THE SCENE WEBSTER

Formal setting. A setting conceived in the simple refinement of a basic motif. In stage settings this type of setting usually suggests architecture, sculpture, or a plastic abstraction of an idea.

Gallery. The area just above the balcony, equipped with seats for spectators.

Garden stage. A natural open-air stage in a garden.

Gauze. A finely woven netting or scrim through which light and form can be seen. Fog, storm, and nebulous effects are gained by the use of gauze, usually in the form of curtains. Gauze is also used in the creation of illusions in light.

Glaze. To apply a thin coat of diluted paint on an already painted surface in order to subtilize and unify the tone; the thin watery paint used to cover flats in a toning process.

Grass mat. A unit of artificial grass used in exterior settings for the stage.

Grid or gridiron. The wooden or metal beamed structure above the stage to and from which scenery is lowered and hoisted into use.

Grip. A stage hand whose work is mainly that of moving scenery on the stage floor.

Ground color. The first coat of paint applied to flats after they have been sized.

Ground row. Any piece of flat scenery resting on the floor and unjoined to any scenic unit at the top—a piece of flat scenery having for its only contacting element the floor of the stage.

Hand props. Small properties carried on stage by actors.

Hanger iron. A metal stage device fastened to scenery and equipped with rings for hooking on a snatch line.

Hanging scenery. Any unit of scenery suspended and controlled from the gridiron as opposed to scenery which rests on the stage floor and is shifted offstage; for example, a drop, border, or overhead effect.

High light. To paint the suggestion of light on paneled objects or to paint the area around a light to agree with its intensity; the part of an object that receives direct light.

House. The auditorium of a theatre.

House lights. The lights used to illuminate the auditorium.

Hue. The predominance of a certain light ray (integrally a part of white light) recognized in the reflection given back by an object, the aesthetic effect of which causes an observer immediately to classify the color under a definite name. For example, a red hue or a green hue.

Intensity. The degree of brightness or saturation of a hue. For example, a brilliant orange, a dull blue, an intense violet. Comparison should be with identical color, brilliant orange, dull orange, etc.

Jack. A wooden device usually triangular in shape used to support ground rows, cutouts, or other scenic units; the upright part of the brace should in most cases be constructed at slightly less than a right angle in order that security in the bracing can be gained by the leaning of the unit.

Keep alive. To store or pack flats so that they are readily available.

Keeper hook. An S-shaped iron device slipped over toggle bars of adjacent flats into which a horizontal batten is slipped to maintain one plane throughout.

Keystone. A three-ply wooden unit used to join wooden members of flats together by means of clout nails.

Lash. To fasten one flat to another by means of a lash line and cleats.

Lash line. A light rope used for fastening adjacent flats together, usually sash cord.

Lash line cleat. A device used on the sides of two adjacent flats at alternate heights to guide a lash line; special stage hardware.

Lay-in. To apply general preliminary colored paint to a setting. In painting scenery, the first step after sizing; the first layer of color on scenery.

Left stage. The area of the stage to the left of a center line from the point of view of one facing the audience.

Lifting jack. A device for lifting a roller unit used in shifting scenery.

Light pocket. A spot within the lighted area where there is no light; a light void.

Lock off. To clamp shut the lock controlling the endless line in a counterweight system.

Long line. That line of a set of rigging lines which goes from the pin rail to the far side of the stage.

Long load. Flats over sixteen feet when transported are considered a "long load" requiring a special truck or wagon.

Louvres. Circular strips of metal used in a certain type of lighting instrument for the purpose of sending out the light in parallel rays.

Macbeth trap. A trap in the stage floor which may be quickly opened or closed.

Mahl stick. A wooden rod or stick tipped with a cloth pad held in one hand while painting in order to guide the "brush hand."

Manager. In Elizabethan times the individual of the theatre who wrote, adapted, or bought plays and directed them. Modern times have little changed this definition.

Mask. To hide or conceal the "top works," the permanent stage walls, or anything on the stage from view of the audience.

Middle line. The rigging line from the pin rail to the center of a batten.

Mise-en-scène. The French word meaning the active process of setting the stage or putting a production upon the stage.

Mood. "Temper or mind, tone or disposition of consciousness, the sum of which gives the dominant emotional character or cast of mind." (*Webster's International Dictionary.*) In scenery, the emotional feeling expressed by an element of stage production; the emotional feeling accompanying an actor, composition, play, scene, or anything on the stage during performance.

Motif. A symbol of expression. In drawing, a basic line, shape, or unit of pattern. In scenery, a dominant pictorial unit for the graphic or emotional expression of a theatrical idea.

Naturalism. A modern movement in scenic design which calls for the use of truthful detail in expressing surface realism in play production (a late stage in the development of realistic scenery). Settings of this type are generally crowded with many real objects and details and, although the ensemble effect is not as artificial as the older style of painted realism, there is still a great gap between this form and simplified realism or expressionistic stylization.

Olivet. A type of lighting instrument in general use. It consists of a square metal hood containing a 1,000-watt bulb. It is used to illuminate large areas and is adjustable either in a floor stand or as a hanging instrument.

Pack or scene pack. Flats stacked side by side, edges out. Thus, a scene dock may contain a number of packs.

Paint frame. A wooden frame, usually adjustable in height, used for painting scenery.

Parallel. A collapsible supporting structure which combined with a portable floor forms a platform; the supporting element of a platform.

Pattern. In design, an orderly composition of forms.

Perspective. The pictorial illusion or representation of depth, thickness, or the third dimension of an object or group of objects.

Perspective sketch. A drawing of a stage setting fully visualized, in all details, and represented with relation to the illusions of perspective and light.

Picture frame hook. A hook screwed into the back of a picture or small fixture. This hook slips into a picture frame socket.

Pigment (paint). Color or substance in its basic form.

Pin-rail. An iron rail equipped with cleats for making fly lines fast.

Plan. Any diagrammatic drawing showing the position, shape, scale, and measure of the stage setting in detail. A plan generally including all openings, practical features, backings, off-stage units, furniture, and principal properties. This kind of diagram is drawn to scale.

Plastic stage. A stage in which the floor assumes a unified and definite form of unevenness or irregularity; a specially designed stage for a particular production built partially or wholly above the regular stage; a stage the intrinsic line and mass of which form part of the physically decorative effect with the actors and light, and one that is capable of supporting actors in every area.

THE SCENE WEBSTER

Platform. Any supporting structure higher than the stage floor generally used for acting.

Plug. Any scenic detail or unit which fits into or tightly against any opening or aperture in the visual setting.

Practical. A term used to describe any unit of scenery that is purposely moved, adjusted, or mechanically operated by the actor within vision of the audience; any scenic unit capable of bearing weight or strain of actors.

Practical unit. Any piece of scenery devised for the actual use of actors or adjustable by the actor when in use; a trick scenic device, for example, a door that swings or slides, a window that opens, a secret door.

Primaries of light. The term applied to the three basic hues that go to make the spectral equivalent of white lights, i.e., red, green, and blue.

Primaries of pigment. The name given to the three generally accepted basic hues of pigmentary color; i.e., red, yellow, and blue.

Property. Any piece of furniture or any practical or decorative unit used within the area of a setting or detachable from the walls or ceiling thereof.

Proscenium. The vertical architectural structure dividing the stage and the auditorium.

Proscenium arch. The lineal frame characterizing the visual opening of the stage.

Rail. Any external horizontal wooden member of a scenic flat.

Rake. To draw in or slant the upstage ends of the side walls of a setting toward the center of the upstage.

Ramp. An inclined platform of a grade suitable to the actual support of the actor.

Régie. A technical stage term of French origin, used especially in Germany, to denote every element used in play production apart from business management of the theatre. Sheldon Cheney defines it as the work of placing the play in the scene.

Régisseur. The individual of the German theatre who is responsible for the artistic phase of theatrical production; the master-director. His work consists of training actors and conducting rehearsals; he controls the technical accomplishments of the stage and supervises the fusion of theatrical elements into unified production. He is the dictator as long as the play goes on. In France he is the resident stage manager appointed and paid by the administration.

Revolving stage. A circular platform upon different sections of which all the different scenes within a play are erected in a more or less permanent manner. This stage requires careful planning of scenery, especially in so far as masking and ingenious utility is concerned.

Rhythm. The visual effect given by the regularly recurrent use of a basic motif in a stage setting; a pleasing variety in visual design. In general, movement marked by regular recurrence.

Right stage. The area of the stage to the right of a center line from the point of view of one facing the audience.

Riser. The vertical part or height of a structural step.

Roll ceiling. A ceiling which by the removal of its shorter wooden supports can be rolled on the longer ones in the manner of a scroll.

Run a flat. To move a flat in an upright position by sliding the forward part of it. By special manipulation a single stage hand is capable of moving a heavy or tall flat.

Scale. The relationship of one object to another as established by comparing an object of unknown quality such as size, width, et cetera, with an object of known size, width, et cetera.

Scenery. Technically speaking, that part of the setting which incloses the acting area. This definition is given in order to distinguish between properties and scenery for stage crews.

Sculptured stage. A formal type of stage, the aesthetic effect of which resembles sculptured forms.

Scumbling. The application of a studied, dry-brush stroke of color to the ground color of a setting. This is accomplished by touching the flat gently with the end of a brush not too full of paint.

Set up. To assemble a setting.

Shade. That part of an object which is neither in direct light nor in shadow. Also, in color, a variation of a hue, darker than the hue at full intensity.

Shadow. The dark visual image caused by the obstruction of an object in the path of light rays.

Shift. To remove one scene and set up another.

Short line. The rigging line from the pin-rail to the nearest end of a batten.

Side wall. The wall on each side of the stage.

Sill iron. A piece of narrow-gauge iron used across the bottom of a door or opening flat for purposes of support.

Size. To apply a mixture of whiting, glue, and water to new flats or scenic units prior to the actual painting of the setting.

Sky dome. A permanently constructed plaster inclosure regularly curved around its two sides, rear, and top, painted and used in combination with light to represent the sky and other effects. In some theatres a sky dome is used instead of a cyclorama.

Smoke doors. Doors in the roof above the grid, held shut by a cut line. In case of fire these doors are opened, drawing the fire up, and thus helping to prevent its spread to the auditorium.

Smoke pockets. Iron guides for the asbestos curtain which, in case of fire, half prevents smoke and flame from getting into the auditorium.

Snatch line. A line suspended from a batten and equipped with a small hook for use in fastening it to a piece of scenery.

Space stage. A stage in which abstract space becomes part of the pictorial composition.

Spatter. The application of dots of color on the ground color of a setting, caused by hitting the ferule of the brush against the opposite wrist and causing dots of color to spatter upon the setting.

Spot line. A line hung from the grid to hit a particular spot on the stage floor.

Stage brace. An adjustable brace used to support flats or other scenic units from the rear.

Stage carpenter. The stage craftsman whose principal duty it is to make out and assemble, set up, and strike the stage setting.

Stage hand. The worker behind the scenes; a shifter of scenery; the machinist of the theatre.

Stage machinery. Any mechanical contrivance designed to expedite scene shifting.

Strike. To remove a setting or any scenic unit or article from the stage. A term used in shifting scenes.

Tab backing. A drop or curtain lowered behind a tab curtain.

Teaser. A curtain, drop, border, or permanent architectural structure used horizontally to establish the height of the actual proscenium opening. In most cases this is adjustable.

Template bench. A square frame elevated for convenient use in the making of quantities of uniform flats, especially by the mortise and tenon method. Such a device insures uniformity in angles and sizes.

Thickness piece. The narrow flats forming the thickness of scene openings. For example, the thickness of an arch or doorway.

Three-fold. Three flats or screens hinged so as to fold together.

Tie off. To make fast a fly line to the pin-rail. To close the lock of a counterweight unit.

Toggle bar. Any vertical or horizontal member of a flat inclosed within the outside frame.

Toning of color. Bringing of colors or variations together by means of mixing adjacent colors while wet or by the use of water or glaze.

Tormentors. The flats or permanent architectural sides of a proscenium opening used to establish the width of the setting at its downstage extremity. In the case of flats the tormentors allow an adjustable width.

Trapped area. The section of the stage floor equipped with removable section traps.

Tread. The horizontal part or width of a step.

Trimming. The process of hanging drops or borders so that the lower edge is parallel to the stage floor.

Tripping. The process of raising the lower edge of a drop so that it is even with the upper edge, thus diminishing the drop to half of its former height. This is called tripping, and the drop a tripping drop. This method provides an easy way to mask drops on a small stage with a low grid.

Two-fold. Two flats or screens hinged so as to fold together.

Upstage. The rear area of the stage within the visual setting; the term applied to the direction of an actor as he moves away from the footlights.

Value. In painting, the degree of darkness or lightness of a color in terms of a color scale ranging from white to black. To determine the value of a color one should squint the eye almost shut, thus eliminating the effect of the hue and reducing the color to a neutral effect.

Vehicle. The liquid used to flow or dissolve pigment or substance.

Vibrate. To create a moving effect in color, light, or pattern.

Visual setting. That part of a physical setting within the sight lines of anyone in the audience.

Wagon stage. A stage equipped with horizontal runways for wagons or trucks upon which settings are placed, rolled into position on the stage proper, and, when finished, rolled to the opposite side for striking, resetting, or storage. In the more modern wagon stages the trucks are sometimes pivoted downstage right and left instead of being rolled on and off. The wagon stage is a practical mechanical manner of quickly changing scenery.

Walk it up. Method of raising a flat from a horizontal to a vertical position.

Warm color. A hue which reveals a predominantly positive emotional effect. Any chromatic variation ranging from yellow at one extreme through orange and red to red-violet at the other extreme.

Window flat. A flat containing an opening for a window and frame; a flat containing a window.

Wing nut. A nut having small "wings" so that it may be easily turned with the fingers.

Wings. Flats set at either side of the stage, parallel to the footlights, covering off the sides of the stage from the view of the audience.

Wood wing. An irregularly shaped wing representing part of a wood or rustic scene.

Working drawings. Drawings made by the draftsman from the artist's sketch for use in scene construction.

INDEX

Acting areas, 32; definition, 83; lighting of, 49
Action, setting adapted to, 19
Actor, focality of, 3; highlighting, 47; illumination of, 44, 45, 49; moods of, 81; shadow of, 42, 47
American Tragedy, An, 62
Angle irons, 78
Ansky, S., *The Dybbuk*, 6; sketches for, 6, 7, 40
Appia, Adolphe, 44, 80
Architectural detail, 4, 18, 20, 29; effects, 41; Greek, 79; materials for, 34; painting, 59 f.; Roman, 79; stage, 82
Architecture, 8, 9, 23
Artificial flowers and trees, 65
Artist, 83; scene model for, 32; tools and materials, 58
Atmosphere, 83; background, 4; emotional, 37; of fantasy, 51; of mystery play, 3, 9, 29; period, 45–46; suggested by design, 5
Auditorium, fan-shaped, 19; size of, 14

Backdrop, 12, 15, 36, 41, 46, 66, 74, 75, 82
Back flap, 83
Backstage construction, 21
Bailey, Dr. Margery, xi
Baker, George Pierce, 13; production by, 46
Balcony, 14, 83; sight lines from, 20, 24
Barber, Philip, xi
Bassett, Professor Lee Emerson, xi
Batten, 42, 83
Belasco, David, 44
Bellows, George, 28
Bevan, Frank Poole, xi; design by, 64
Bohemian Club, San Francisco, Christmas Play, 45; Rafetto's, 1930, 58
Book-ceiling, 83
Border, 83; light, 44
Botanical effects, 62
Box-setting, 14, 18, 80, 83; cost of, 74
Brangwyn, Frank, 28
Browne, Maurice, 70
Budget, 13, 14, 72–73; depends on number of performances, 72
Budgeting, 75
Business manager, 13, 86

Candlelight in the theatre, 40
Čapek, Karel, *The Makropolous Secret*, 5; setting for, 5, 24, 50
Cathcart, Robert, xi

Ceiling, *see* Book-ceiling, Roll ceiling
Chastelard, by Swinburne, 15, 16
Chekhov, *The Marriage Proposal*, 48
Cheney, Sheldon, 81, 87
Chromatic changes in scenery, 40, 49
Church setting, 79
Circus operetta, setting for, 56
Clark, Barrett H., xi
Clavilux, 43
Clugston, Katherine, *Finished*, setting for, 74
Color, 4, 7, 9, 31; keynote to emotion, 31; in lighting, 45, 49; monochromatic, 51; of setting, 23; sketch, 83; subordination of, 15
Color charts, 9, 52
Comedy, 11; mood of, 3, 31, 55; revival of Restoration, 45
Constructivistic production, 3, 83
Constructivists, 80, 83
Control board, 36, 44; model, 37
Convertible scenery, painting, 57 f.
Cost of construction, 21, 72 ff.; analysis of, 72; economy, 72 ff.
Costumes, 15, 16, 22; cost of costuming, 72; knowledge of costuming, 9
Covarrubias, 28
Cradle, 84
Craig, Gordon, 13, 44, 80, 81
Creation, scene from, 43
Creative stage of scene design, 23
Cross sections, 21 f., 84
Cushing, *The Devil in the Cheese*, iv, 3; design for, 65
Cyclorama, 15, 67, 84; black, 50; light upon, 41, 46; painting of, 37, 40; sky, 66; substitute for, 36; trough, 41, 42, 84

Dance, 8; drama, 43
Dane, Clemence, *Granite*, setting for, 47
Davis, Gordon, xi, 30; productions, 57
Dean, Alexander, 48
Decor, 84
Designer, scene, 84; artist and craftsman, 8; execution by, 10, 30; experimenting, 9; knowledge of architecture, 9; qualifications, 8–9; technical manager, 9
Dimming, control boards, 37
Direct charges, 72 ff.
Director, 8, 9, 13, 84; and style of production, 11, 12
Distortion, 18, 42, 43

— 91 —

Downstage, 84
"Draw," class, 14
Draw curtain, 83
Drawings or sketches, 33; aesthetic, 17, 27; execution of, 8, 9, 10, 33; floor plans, 18, 19; imagination in, 8, 27; media, 26; paper for, 17; to scale, 18, 22; of sight lines, 20; simplicity, 28; technical, 17; working, 17 ff.
Dripping, 56
Duffy, Vincent, 74
Dulac, Edmund, 27

Earth colors, 84
Economy, 13; in building, 21; in cost of construction and materials, 72 ff.
Elevations, 9, 20 f.; drawings of, 21
Elevator stages, 13, 36
Emotional keynote, 16, 31; lighting and, 43
Entrances, 9, 32, 45
Equipment, electrical, 75; permanent, 75
Evreinov, *The Chief Thing*, 51; sketch of setting for, 51
Experts, modern lighting, 44
Expressionistic presentation, 3
Expressionists, 80, 84
Exterior setting, 23, 36, 61 f.; architectural, 68; lighting, 44; see Botanical effects

Fantasies, dramatic, 61, 66
Farce, 11, 12
Fields and marshes, 66
Flanagan, Hallie, 48
Flashlight, 48
Flats, 18, 84; hinged, 35; painting, 54; running, 87
Flood lights, 45, 47
Floor plan, 18, 19; in pencil and wash, 19
Flowers, artificial, 61, 62, 64; plants and, 63
Flowers, Priscilla, *The White Peacock*, settings for, 41, 54
Flylines, 33, 84
Foot irons, 78, 84
Frames, materials for, 34; for painting scenery, 53, 54, 86
Furniture, 20, 25, 58; painting, 58 f.

Gallery, 14, 85
Gauze, theatrical, 41, 85
Gilbert and Sullivan, *The Pirates of Penzance*, 62
Glazing, 57, 85
Gnesin, Maurice, *The Rendezvous of the Unknown Soldier*, model settings for, 34
Grass, 62; mat, 85; painted, 62
Greek drama, 79
Greek theatre, colored light in, 40; lighting of, 39, 40; stage in, 79
Green, Paul, *The Last of the Lowries*, setting for, 14
Gridiron (or grid), 15, 33, 85; counterweight system, 15; with flylines, 33; height of, 46; old style, 15

Ground color, 85; see Ground tone
Ground row, 12, 41, 46, 78, 84
Ground tone, 57, 59, 84
Guérin, Jules, 28

Hall, George, 36
Hamlet, periodized, 13; models for, 35
Hanging scenery, 85
Hardware, 15, 36, 74, 77; stage, 78
Hartman, Louis, 44
Hasait, light projections, 43
Hasenclever, *Wanted: A Gentleman*, sketch for, 73
Helvenston, Harold, designs by, iv, 12, 18, 22, 25, 30, 39, 43, 47, 48, 51, 53, 54, 57, 58, 74, 75; drawings of elevations, 21, 22; mystery play by, 38; plays directed by, 70; productions by, 60; plugging board by, 37; settings by, 5, 12, 24, 26, 33
Hilar production, 3
Holzmuller, Charles, 44
Homer, Winslow, 27
Hopkins-Jones production, 3
Humphrey, Maude, *The Singing Minute*, a scene from, 48
Hurt, Arthur, xi; lighting by, 35; models by, 35

Ibsen, *Brand*, setting for, 22; lighting, 43; scenic demands, 40 f.; *The Vikings of Heligoland*, 43; *The Wild Duck*, sketch and setting for, 30
Ideas, 22, 23; symbols of, 27
Illumination, 49 f.; see Lighting
Illusion, of sky, 23; see Projections in light
Impressionistic effect, 14
Instruments, lighting, 16, 42; exposed, 46; miniature, 44; model, 37; position of, 46
Interior lighting, 44; scenes introduced, 80

Jennings, Talbot, *No More Frontier*, setting for, 69
Jones, Robert Edmond, 39, 81
Jorgulesco, Jonel, 43
Jungles and forests, 66

Kent, Mrs. William, Jr., 41
Keystones, 77, 85
Kirk, E. B., 44
Kline, William, xi; design by, 38, 69

Lash line cleat, 85
"Laying-in," 55, 85
Leg drops, 36, 75
Light, 18, 38 ff.; chromatic changes in scenery by, 40; colored, effect of, 37, 49; dominant factors, 80; in drawings, 27; effect of, 23, 27; emotional expression in, 40; intensity, 46; pockets, 47, 85; projections, 40 f.
Light borders, 44 f.
Light bridge, 48
Light plots, 9

INDEX

Lighting, 69; color and, 4, 7; continuities, 44; cross-, 44, 45; foot-, 44, 45, 46, 50; instruments, 16, 18, 37, 42, 44, 46; level, 44, 45; mechanical devices, 43; miniature equipment, 44; moonlight, 47; mood, 4; obvious, 47, 48; offstage, 46; overhead, 44, 45, 50; period, 45; season, 4; settings under different, 4, 34; subtle, 48 f.; system, model, 33; under-, 46; unified, 17
Lightning, *see* Special effects
Lin, Phyllis, design by, 70
Line and mass, 7, 28; and color, 15, 30, 81; and light, 24, 30
Linnebach, principle, 41; projections by, 43; projector, 41
Little theatres, scenery for, 58
Littleton, Covington, 46
Locale, 4, 13, 70
Louvres, 47, 86

Macbeth, 13; Douglas Ross production, 13
McCandless, Stanley, xi, 44; lighting designed by, 46
McClelland, John, xi
Mahl stick, 86
Makeup, knowledge of, 9
Marble, painting of, 59
Mask-spattering, 57
Materials, 14, 65; cambric, 63; canvas, 15, 65; cost of, 76 ff.; gauze, 41, 85; lumber, 15, 76; for model settings, 37; obviousness of, 28; papier-mâché, 25, 34, 35, 36, 64, 65, 67; permanent stage, 15; for scene painting, 52; silk, 60; stage building, 76 f.; structural, 34, 76; for topographical effects, 67
Melodrama, 11
Milne, *The Ivory Door,* setting for, 60
Miniature stage setting, 35; lighting equipment for, 35, 44; painting of, 33
Miniature theatre, figures for, 37; on model-box, 32, 33; scale of, 33
Model, scene, 32, 33; painting of, 36; plastic, 32; rule for, 33; scaled, 32, 33; settings, 36, 37
Model lighting equipment, 36, 37, 43; substitutes for, 37
Molnár, Ferencz, *Mima,* 4
Mood, defined, 85; design in setting, 7, 9; dramatic, 80, 85; emotional, 6, 11, 44, 51; light and, 30, 40, 43; minor, 44; painting and, 55; setting for, 7
Movement, effect of, 40, 41, 47
Muntins, window, 35, 76
Musical comedy, 11; lighting for, 45; settings for, 12, 18, 62, 72
Musical shows, 50, 66, 73, 75

Newbegin, John, 37
Nichols, Robert, 70; and Maurice Browne, *Wings over Europe,* setting for, 70
Norris, Charles G., xi

Oenslager, Donald, xi; designs by, 42, 46; *The Flying Dutchman,* 42; light projections, 43; *Pueblo,* 46
Offstage, lighting effects, 46
Olivets, 36, 47, 50, 86
O'Neill, Eugene, 40; settings for *The Emperor Jones,* 4, 61; *Beyond the Horizon,* 62
Openings, 9, 18; light from, 47
Opera, comic, 11; Wagnerian, 80
Orchestra, 19; sight lines, 66
Outlining, 57
Ozite, 67

Pack, 86
Pageant, 11; lighting of, 44
Paint, dry color, 52; oil, 52; pulp, 52 f.; water color, 52; *see* Painting
Painting, scene, 51, 53; color and lighting, 49; furniture and properties, 58 f.; key of, 46; materials and equipment for, 52; methods of, 53, 54; of models, 36
Pantomime, 8
Papier-mâché, 25, 34, 35, 36, 64, 65, 67
Pattern, scenic, 13, 23, 24, 25
Peking Politics, by J. Wong-Quincey, 13; settings for, 25, 26, 27
Period, design, 4, 11, 13, 29, 61, 71; historical, 70
Perspective sketch, elements of, 23
Pevear, Munro, 44
Pichel, Irving, 44
Pigment, 86; and colored light, 24, 37, 49, 55; primaries of, 87
Pirandello, *Right You Are,* setting for, 56
Plaster dome, 15, 40, 58
Plastic, or constructivist settings, 32, 33, 64, 86
Plastic units, 37
Porgy, 62
Powell, Robert, *Brief Candle,* 64
Production, traditional, 11; amateur, 72
Projections, 40, 41, 67; in light, 47; shadow, 66
Properties, 17, 18, 22, 87; cost of, 72; painting, 58 f.; special, 29
Proscenium arch, 17, 23, 79, 87; height of, 19; modifications, 12, 47; sight lines through, 32; size of, 14; sketches of, 22

Rackham, Arthur, 27
Rafetto, Michael, setting for Christmas play written for the Bohemian Club, 58
Rail, 87
Raking, 19, 87
Raleigh, Henry, 29
Ramps, 18, 35, 87
Realistic settings, 70, 71, 80
Régie, 87
Reinhardt, Max, 44; lighting, 48
Requisitions, 75
Revolving stage, 36, 87
Revue, 11; cost of, 75; design for, 72; musical, 11, 62, 75

— 93 —

Rice, Elmer, *The Adding Machine*, 4, 43, 74; graveyard setting for, 47; *Street Scene*, 68, 74
Richardson, Eri, Jr., 38
Riser, 87
Road, scenery for the, 14, 15
Roerich, Nicholas, 8
Roll ceiling, 87
Rolling, 55 f.
Ross, Douglas, 13, 81
Rossi, David, 4; designs by, 73
Ruthenberg, Grace Dorcas, *Retreat*, setting for, 70

San Francisco Junior League, *The Sleeping Beauty*, 41
San Francisco Temple Players, 6, 7, 40
Scale, 87; authenticity of, 69
Scene designer, art of, 8 ff.; imaginative art, 13; mounting in charge of, 72; place in theatre, 9; qualifications, 8 f.; salary, 72–73
Scene painting, methods of, 53; finishing, 55 f.; technique, 55
Scenery, 87; as background for actor, 81; convertible, 57 f.; cost of, 72; and costumes, 16; in Greece and Rome, 39, 40, 79; hanging, 85; in Italy, 79; modern, 79; shifting of, 15, 70, 88; size and arrangement, 19; styles of, 79; wagon stage for, 89
Schiller's *Fiasco*, sketch for, 18
Script, 11, 12
Sculpture, 9
Scumbling, 56, 87
Seivert, light projections, 43
Sequence, chromatic, 53; of scenery, 40, 49
Setting, aesthetic effect of, 7; evolution from sketch, 30; attributes of good, 31; model, 33; permanent, 35; stylized, 40, 66, 80; realistic type, 48, 80; scale of, 68
Shadow, of actor, 42, 47; projections, 66
Shakespeare, 40 f., 43; *Hamlet*, 13, 35; *Macbeth*, 13; *Merry Wives of Windsor*, 62
Shapes, stylized, 3
Shaw, Bernard, 40; *Back to Methuselah*, 43; *Saint Joan*, sketch for settings, 14, 33; *Pygmalion*, scene from, 5, 68
Sherwood, *The Queen's Husband*, setting for, 57
Short line, 88
Sight lines, 19, 23; drawings of, 20
Silk, rayon, 60
Simonson, Lee, 43, 81
Sizes, commercial and actual, 77
Sizing, 55
Sketch, evolution of setting from, 30, 31; non-committal qualities, 29
Sky, 23, 35; dome, 88; lighting, 44 f.; trick effects, 47
Smith, Edwin H., xi
Smoke doors, 88
Spattering, 37, 56, 88
Special effects, 40, 47 f., 59; painting, 59, 60, 67

Sponging, 56
Spot line, 88
Spotlight, 43, 47, 49
Stage, box-setting for small, 14; building measurements, 76 f.; crew, 15; design, 8 (*see* Designer); floor, size of, 19; lighting, 9, 39–40; machinery, 88; management, 72; and technician, 14
Stage setting, 12, 13, 24, 26, 27, 30, 41, 47, 56, 58, 64, 70, 74; chromatic elements of, 16, 24; of eighteenth century, 79; evolution of, 31; scale of, 26; sketches for, 4, 6, 7, 12, 14, 15, 16, 30, 31, 42, 47, 51, 53, 59, 73
Stained glass, 60
Stanford University productions, 4, 5, 12, 24, 30, 47, 50, 51, 56, 57, 60, 65, 70
Steininger, Alma, xi, 33
Stone, 60
Storage, mechanical devices for, 36; space for, 15, 65, 75
Stover, Frederick, xi; designs by, 14, 15, 47, 70; settings by, 15, 60, 61, 74
"Striking" scenery, 35, 88
Strip lights, 41, 46
Striping, 57
Strong, Austin, *A Play without a Name*, 3
Style, artist's, 30 f., 71; of director, 3; personal, in settings, 10; of production, 3, 11; in stage scenery, 7, 79
Stylistic technique, 14, 40, 80
Subordination of color, 15
Substitute for cyclorama, 36
Sunlight, 47
Swinburne's *Chastelard*, sketch of unit for, 15, 16
Switchboards, 16, 44, 73

Tableau, 11
Talbot, Mrs. Andrew, 41
Teaser, 33, 88; batten, 42; height of, 19, 23
Technician, 14, 73
Technique, 7, 30, 57
Three-dimensional forms, 18, 59, 74, 80; model, 32
Toggle bar, 88
Toller, *Masse Mensch*, model settings for, 4
Toning, 56
Topographical effects, 67
Tormentors, 19, 23, 33, 41, 42, 88
"Tower, The," sketch for scene from *Chastelard*, 16
Tragedy, 11; sketch for, 31; spirit of, 3, 55
Transparency, 60
Trapped area, 15, 33, 88
Trees and shrubs, 36, 61, 64; "cut-out," 65; model, 36
Trimming, 88
Tristan and Isolde, setting for, 31
Two-dimensional construction, 18, 66
Two-point perspective, 22

INDEX

Units, scenic, 12, 19, 41; circular, 35; cost reckoned on number of, 74; "live," 75, 76; plastic, 37; reversed, 13; scale of, 14; step, 18; "struck" quickly, 35; three-dimensional, 18, 59, 74, 80
Unity of idea, 12
Upstage, 19, 89; lighting, 42

Van Loon, Hendrik, 28
Varnish, 52, 53, 58 f.
Vassar Experimental Theatre, 48
Vehicle, 52, 89
Vines, 62
Visual effect, 36, 89
Visual setting, 89

Wagner, Richard, *The Flying Dutchman*, scenes from, 42; stage lighting, 44
Wagon stage, 36, 89; for scene shifting, 15
Water, 67
Wilfred, Thomas, 43
Wings, 89
Wood, and graining, 59
Working drawings, 89; *see* Drawings

Yale University, Department of the Drama, xi, 4, 13, 39, 41, 44, 46, 48, 54, 64; Fine Arts Ball at, 53

Wong-Quincey, J., 13

Zuloaga, 28
Zorn, Anders, 28

"The goal is far—
True guides are few—
　　But many of these are Books."

　　　　　　　　—Anon.

This book is set in a French face adapted as Linotype No. 16, with Linotype Metro Bold headings. The design is by Hartley Jackson. First publication, June 1931.